PROFILE
POEMS AND STORIES

Also by Armando García-Dávila

Out Of My Heart/De Mi Corazon. Poetry published in English and Spanish by Thumbprint Press. (1999)

At the Edge of the River/Al Lado Del Rio. Prose and poetry published in English and Spanish by Running Wolf Press. (2007)

Works in Other Publications

Poetry and short stories were a regular feature in *La Voz*, a bilingual newspaper.

Bless Me Father for I Have Sinned and *The Pendulum.* Humorous short stories featured in *Bust Out Stories,* a Thumbprint Press magazine.

Healdsburg Alive! Eight Sonoma County Writers Pay Homage to a Great Northern California Town. (2012)

Awards

Bless Me Father for I Have Sinned and *If I Could* were awarded first place blue ribbons at the Marin County Fair. (1998)

Healdsburg, California, Literary Laureate—2002/2003.

"'*La vida contigo es un tango.* Life with you is a tango, / sometimes tricky, sometimes sweaty, always bold, / daring, grace, guts, and comedy!' In 'El Tango,' one of many tributes to the woman he adores, poet and storyteller Armando García-Dávila sums up his artful dance. With love up his sleeve—charming, savvy—he moves across life's floor, hugging his Mexican roots, embracing spirituality. Betrayed by the Catholic Church of his youth, the poet steps back from institutions, trusting instead the tell-tale intimacy of family and community. In 'American God,' a prose-poem, he revisits his questioning childhood. 'Other kids went to church in newer cars, with newer clothes, with newer parents. . . . But if we praised the same God in the same way, then why did He bless *them* so much more than us?' To the beat of one heart, Armando García-Dávila's *Profile* shines a lyric light into America's ballrooms, backyards, and closets."

—AL YOUNG, California's poet laureate emeritus

"This lovely, well-written book of verse and stories touched my heart. These poems and stories travel back and forth in time evoking childhood memories of the Catholic Church paired with a writer's close analysis of the betrayal of innocence and the senselessness of war. However, interwoven throughout these painful moments is a poet's eye for finding those moments in life which also heal. Lines such as 'And the only sounds interrupting this immense meditation would be the wisps of butterfly wings, and a prayerful chant quietly echoing in each canyon.
"Love." "Love." "Love."'
Those words help to remind us, that despite the perplexity of life, there is tremendous power in the transformative act of remembering and being present to the beauty of living."

—IANTHE BRAUTIGAN SWENSEN, author of *You Can't Catch Death* (2001)

"Armando is full of passion and questions as are his dancing words."

—SUSAN SWARTZ, author of *The Juicy Tomatoes Guide to Ripe Living after 50* (2006)

"How wonderful to have in hand this hot book. Call it 'An Armando García-Dávila Reader.' A collection of new and old work, poems, prose poems, and stories, it explores love, death, sex, and labor. The author's voice cries out from the wilderness, laments the loss of faith and celebrates the renewal of faith in poems that shock, arouse, and evoke the beauty of earthly and heavenly bodies and extoll the earth itself. *In Profile: Poems and Stories*, García-Dávila reveals himself as a dreamer waking to the agony and the ecstasy of life, rousing and arousing readers from sleep, from forgetfulness and from their own addictions."

—JONAH RASKIN, author of *Rock 'n' Roll Women* (2012) and *A Few French Scenes* (2013)

"A writer's heart displayed is a beautiful thing, especially when the view includes honesty, courage, and wisdom. In his new book, *Profile*, Armando García-Dávila shows us the passionate, loving, laughing, angry, proud, and wise heart that beats in his chest. At first flush these forty-seven poems and seven stories feel safe and warm, like Armando's studio on a hilltop in Santa Rosa, until you realize the risks he takes—and asks us to take—in many of his pieces.

'Want to be free?' Armando asks. 'Lay your ego by the side of the road and in your sternest voice give the command, "Stay!" Then run like hell until you can't hear its protests anymore.'

In 'The Muse,' Armando writes: 'Poetry barged through my door one day. . . . When in good humor, she gave herself without pause or shame, and the verses flowed freely. . . . Other times she ripped a tooth from my jawbone in barter for a single line.'

Armando's love poems do what the finest of that genre always have: make us feel what we're called upon to give and receive to call ourselves human. Armando is a Sonoma County treasure, and in the world I want to live in he'd be a treasure in all of California and beyond, wherever the young, the sensitive, the passionate, the hungry, the hurt, the abandoned, and the brave demand respect and truth."

—DAVID BECKMAN, author of *Language Factory of the Mind* (2012)

PROFILE

POEMS AND STORIES

Armando García-Dávila

McCaa Books • Santa Rosa

McCaa Books
1604 Deer Run
Santa Rosa, CA 95405-7535

Copyright © 2014 by Armando García-Dávila
All Rights Reserved

Without limiting the rights under copyright reserved above, no part of this publication may be reproduced, distributed, or transmitted in any form or by any means, or stored in a database or retrieval system, without the prior written permission of both the copyright owner and the publisher of this book except in the case of brief quotations embodied in critical articles or reviews.

ISBN 978-0-9960695-0-2
First published in 2014 by McCaa Books,
an imprint of McCaa Publications.

Printed in the United States of America
Set in Minion Pro

www.mccaabooks.com

To Kathy who has always been there for me. "I love you more than I could ever express, sweetheart."

To Doris whose financial and emotional support has made this possible. "I love and miss you."

CONTENTS

    Preface   13

Poems

  The Day Will Come   17
  Dead List   18
  Distracted   20
  A Free Man   22
  If I Could   23
  J.C.   25
  Lonely   26
  Mother Sea   27
  October Corn   30
  Roadside Flowers   33
  Two Springs   34
  The Herd   36
  The Muse   37
  The Pit   39
  Where Are You?   41
  120/80   43
  Carry Me   45
  The Greatest Poem   47
  You've Got Mail   48
  A Respite   51
  Could You Love Me?   52
  Embers   53

An Exquisite Eve	54
Her Song	55
If I Loved You Yesterday	56
Listen	57
Of Little Boys and Kisses	58
Of Love and Uncertainty	59
Loving Her	60
Mi Leona	61
Regular Love	62
Silence	63
El Tango	64
A Winter's Alcove	65
Wishing	66
Your Light	67
"Yes!"	68
American God	70
The *Campesinos' Maestra*	71
El Jardinero	73
El Paletero	75
El Gran Viento	76
Monks of the Field	78
El Otro Lado	80
Fresas	82
Which Foot?	83
Wild Flowers	85

Stories

Bless Me Father for I Have Sinned	89
Don't Fall Asleep	97
Chato's Steal	100
Voice Behind the Wall	106
Portrait of a Rose	114
Lord, Snow, and Dawn	120
Love at First Sight	133
Acknowledgments	137
About the Author	139

PREFACE

WHAT FOLLOWS IN THIS BOOK are some revelations of my life and soul through a few poems and short stories. I have no pretensions to seek your understanding or forgiveness. I only hope you enjoy the pathos, sense of seeking, and humor in my work.

The Catholic Church and our family's Mexican roots and modest means provided the foundation of my young years. I remain indebted to my parents, older brother, twin brother, and four sisters for the core of my being. Without them, I would be but a shadow.

However, the church confused me early in life as I came to realize the fallibility of the institution. My intention in writing about it is not to offend but to simply offer its effects on me as an innocent and malleable child.

        Armando García-Dávila
        April 2014

Poems

POEMS

The Day Will Come

And the day will come when you hit the switch,
    but the room will remain dark.

Computers will not hum, monitors will not glow,
    and boys will have no flashing games to play.

Gas pumps will remain silent, and we will
    be forced to walk.

Those who don't know how to start a fire will
    be cold.

The comfortably wealthy will be greatly
inconvenienced.

And those who live under bridges will not notice
    the difference.

PROFILE

Dead List

Black, cold, still outdoors, storm clouds shroud the sunrise. A dove perches in the apple tree outside my kitchen window. A solitary "coo" escapes her beak. I look up and bid her my usual "good morning," wondering if she will sing today with the sky so dark.

Steam rises from my coffee cup; first sip tastes best. I'm always intrigued reading obituaries in the morning paper; entire lives reduced to a handful of words.

"I check da dead list," Tony, my neighbor used to say. He was a World War I veteran, fought for Italy. "Name not on list. Good day today!" I was saddened when his name finally appeared. I miss him. He made me laugh, his irreverence toward the pope, his telling me that my back spasms were because I wasn't "getting enough." The man in me laughed, the altar boy embarrassed.

Sad when the old die, tragic when they're young. Saw an infant's coffin carried by a single pallbearer at a funeral once. And Philip, my best friend in the sixth grade, died one rainy afternoon. The cave he had been digging collapsed in on him. Ma showed me his obituary. Strange seeing his desk empty in our classroom the next day. Grief-stricken, his mother collapsed at the memorial service.

And last year a young woman's husband made the dead list. He was a soldier killed in the war, she pregnant with their first, named the boy after his father.

Endless this checking of dead lists. The lists from Thermopylae, from Waterloo, Bull Run, Normandy, Da Nang, Baghdad, too many to name.

And we will not be seeing the coffins bearing America's colors return home. No day of mourning for them. Each blood sacrifice reduced to an item in the obits.

I consider making another cup of coffee, but lightning explodes overhead. My kitchen turns dark. Glasses in the cupboards rattle. Thunder roars through the valley, shattering the predawn peace. Hail mercilessly pounds the apple tree. Countless blossoms fall to the ground, fruit never to be realized.

And I hear nothing more from the dove.

PROFILE

Distracted

The rising sun bears witness to the commotion of our hectic lives each day. Thunderous machines tear down and rebuild cities, repair streets, as we race to work amid racing engines and honking horns. Helicopters hover high overhead advising us of road conditions that could make us late; we need to hurry. Our car radios fill our ears with happy announcers, happy music, happy advertisers that make us laugh, make us want.

Employers, important appointments, churches, and families compete for our precious time.

And we don't dare miss our television programs. I'm pulling for the pretty young lady vying to be the next singing idol.

We roar at the stadium as the ball soars across the field like a bird on the wing. Oh, what a play!

You understand that it's hard for us to hear much else, don't you?

We do have feelings about the issue though. You know the one about *our* war in *your* country. We see it on the news, your homes turned to rubble, you weeping for your children who have been consumed by fire and hate. And our young warriors who have lost their legs, their arms, their sanity, as one politician screams into his opponent's deaf ear.

This incessant ranting and uproar frightens and confuses us. We close our eyes and ears to it lest it drives us mad. We turn to sedatives and wine for a blissful moment of serenity in our harried and lonely lives.

But after the sun has set on our frenzied world, and the moon has made its way high into the dark night, and it is so still that even the crickets have quieted, and at long last there is a moment of solitude, this is when the dreaded question begins haunting our troubled sleep.

"What, in the name of God, are we doing?"

Then mercifully the alarm clock shrieks and the din begins anew.

PROFILE

A Free Man

Want to be a free man? It's simple. Start by shedding your clothes. They say too much about who you wish to be.

Next, to eliminate the compulsion to dominate, remove your testicles and set them on a shelf out of reach.

Lay your ego by the side of the road and in your sternest voice give the command, "Stay!" Then run like hell until you can't hear its protests.

Erase your history so that you are not a man anymore, nor Catholic, Protestant, Jew, or Muslim. You aren't Mexican, German, or Chinese.

Don't consider the future; in fact, so you won't think at all, put your brain in the freezer (thinking is overrated).

Find a clock and smash it between two stones, then feel your way through days and nights.

Forgive yourself and your children for not being enough. Forgive your ex, forgive God for not giving you the answers you think He owes you.

Now find a place in the shade, and listen to everyone, particularly children and birds. Sit quietly until you recognize the miracle of breath.

If I Could

If only for a moment, I would silence the world's motors, and the roar of the airplane would not be so much as a hum, and the thunder of the locomotive would become less than a moan.

No blaring horns, no screeching brakes, no screaming police sirens would come from the avenue. The din of Industry would cease, and the factory would fall into a coma. Its smoke would lift, allowing the forest to inhale deeply, and once again we would drink from the river.

The miracles of the dawn and the dusk would reclaim their sacred stillness.

The parrot would stop his incessant squawking, and children would play a game of statues. The wino, realizing the gift of his existence, would leave his bottle corked.

The right would swing to the left, and the left would not know where to turn. Politicians would be left without plots to hatch, and the devil, he would run out of tricks.

PROFILE

Shouts would turn to whispers, whispers to thoughts, and thoughts to prayer. Chicks, in their nests, would sleep. And in every canton and hamlet, in every town and city, one would hear only the rhythmic breathing of deep slumber and the throbbing of his own heart. And the only sounds interrupting this immense meditation would be the wisps of butterfly wings, and a prayerful chant quietly echoing in each canyon.

"Love."   "Love."   "Love."

J.C.

I didn't ask You to die for me. Maybe You should've been a carpenter instead of a preacher. Would the world be any different if You had? Would the Crusaders have killed in the name of someone else instead?

Your mother would have been spared the anguish of seeing her son tortured to death. Wouldn't that have been better? You could have given her grandchildren who would have delighted her in her old age, and I would have been spared the guilt of causing Your agony.

I didn't ask You to die for me.

PROFILE

Lonely

No one knocks on my door. No one calls me on the phone. There were no notes left on my porch today, nor a letter in the mail.

A nutshell lies on the ground, its meat stolen by an uncaring squirrel.

I heated my dinner and ate. It was quietly good. I will retire, my bed will be warmed solely by my body.

Tomorrow I will eat breakfast, make a lunch, and go to labor. When I return, I will listen to *Moonlight Sonata*,

and no one

will knock

on my door.

Mother Sea

Swell, break, crash — swell, break, crash.

Cells morph into plankton in Mother Sea, plankton to fish, fish to amphibians to reptiles, mammals, into you, into me. We owned gills once, or did they own us? And what of this dream of being able to breathe underwater. A dream? Or a primal memory?

Swell, break, crash — swell, break, crash.

Mother Sea taps the universe's rhythm at her shores.

Phoenicians, Egyptians, Greeks, and Persians explored and conquered by learning to navigate her waters. South China Sea to The Sea of Galilee, Chinese on their junks, Palestinians and Jews in their modest boats, Altus in the frigid Arctic, Brazilians at a sweltering equator, all go about their daily trade of drawing sustenance from her rich stores, by hand, with basket, spear, hook, and net. Oh Mother Sea from whom all good things come, give us this day our daily fish.

Children run screaming from a rushing shore-break, then gleefully chase it back, not noticing the globe's grand arcing horizon, unaware that the entire world lies there at their feet. Lovers on a white sandy beach lie on a blanket basking in the sun, "by the sea, by the sea, by the beautiful sea."

PROFILE

And in the sea it shall be finished. Minute krill by the million are filtered out in the jowls of colossal baleen whales. A horseshoe crab emerges from a tide pool; its life quickly ends in a sandpiper's beak. A woman paces a widow's walk, looks out to the sea praying for the sight of her man's returning trawler. A wife lays her husband's ashes into the surf.

Roman, Spanish, British mariners, admirals and seamen, captains and oarsmen, whalers and their crews, have all tasted the sea's salt, and lost to "the deep" in storm and war. Once mighty armadas, royal galleons of timber, sail, and flaming cannon, countless slave ships, and fleets of cargo ships, ships of hardened iron, and deafening engines, their holds laden rich with silk, oil, grain, and ore, are now scores upon scores of rusting skeletons, linking continents like highways of death, across the ocean's cold silent bed.

Swell, break, crash — swell, break, crash.

Patiently, relentlessly, wave by wave, minute-by-minute, by day and night, and into the millennia, Mother Sea pounds rock coasts to sand. When agitated she spins sky above, assails the land with gale wind and torrential rain, claiming city and village, claiming forest and earth, man and beast alike, drawing all to her watery bosom.

Remember man that thou art of the sea, and unto the sea thou shalt return. The sea gives, and the sea takes.

Swell, break, crash — swell, break, crash.

Blessed be the name of Mother Sea.

PROFILE

October Corn

The corn stalks in my vegetable garden, a deep green not long ago, have yellowed with age. Once straight, tall, and virile, they are now bent and twisted like decrepit old men. Tomato plants are stressed by fall's chilly night air, and those tomatoes left on the vine will not ripen. It pains me seeing summer's sweetness slowly fading away, but it's all a part of the plan, you know; one's strength giving way to aching bones.

My twin, Fernando, and I went trick or treating as little ones. Tony, our big brother, dressed us as pirates. I got an eye-patch, Fernando a handkerchief tied around his head. Tony made us wooden swords and had me go shirtless into the night. He said real pirates braved the cold, and so I did and didn't allow myself to shiver. Our older sisters took us house-to-house, neighborhood to neighborhood, in a frenzied drive for as much candy as we could gather; pirates pilfering booty. Only Christmas surpassed Halloween in fun, and getting something good for simply being young. These days I'm preoccupied with the business of supporting my family and home.

Newspapers tell me the last of the apples and grapes are being harvested as our country's latest war reaps our young soldiers, squandering funds that could be used to feed the hungry, clothe the naked, and cure the sick. It saddened me to read that Paul Newman died. They say he was old and sick, though I only knew him to be young, handsome, and generous. Someone wrote a poem about his life the next day. I'm glad to see that a poet wrote about something that mattered.

My *Tia* Sara, a grandaunt who lived in Mexico, died when I was a boy. She was old, and wrinkled as a prune. She wore dark ankle-length dresses and flesh-colored stockings that covered what little skin that might be exposed. Her long hair was always braided into a pair of long, gray snakes that were wrapped tight against her scalp. She went to bed one night never to rise again. Ma's cousin, my *Tia* Concha, washed Sara's lifeless body and hair, combed and braided her hair, powdered her face, applied rouge and stuffed wads of newspaper in her mouth to fill her cheeks sunken by death's cold hand. The family had a traditional *"velorio"* for Sara. They laid her out surrounded by candles in her living room. Everyone knelt and prayed for her soul. My uncles dug her grave, and buried her the next day. She received a proper memorial service, even if she was a gossip who constantly doled out advice that hadn't been asked for. My Ma and Pa, and most of my uncles and aunts, have passed on, irreplaceable losses. It saddens me that they are not with me anymore. At least they come to visit with me in dreams once in a while. I take comfort knowing that we will be together again one day.

PROFILE

I love the Day of the Dead, a custom rooted in ancient Mexico. A good way to honor those who have passed to the other world, a way to accept and even poke fun at death, instead of fearing him; a good way to prepare for our own inevitable appointment with him. We can fear or laugh and accept him, for in the end there's no choice in the matter. It's all a part of the deal. Aren't we like stalks of corn? Small tender sprouts in spring, strong and sturdy in summer, frail in autumn, dried and lifeless in winter.

Let us be like the Mexican *Calaveras*, the skeletons who play music, dance and sing, replacing fear with a fiesta. Let us celebrate then, for today we are on this side of the great divide, honoring those on the other, and hoping that one day, we will be remembered in a respectful manner, even if we are imperfect. Raise your cups of *atole*, of *chocolate caliente*, raise your *pan dulce*. Here's to life *mis hermanos y hermanas*, here's to death.

Roadside Flowers

See how they brighten the sterile ground of the byway.

Are they not a testament to beauty in this rushed world of asphalt and automobiles?

Can one not help but see them, and think if only for a moment, that there is so much more than one's quick life of appointments and destinations, which after all, will only be forgotten the very next day?

See how these delicate blossoms adorn the small white cross reminding you that a profound event took place on this spot that you pass each day on your way to seemingly important business.

"Someone made an unforeseen and final stop here," they whisper into each driver's ear.

And all that is left to a man are his humble roadside flowers, and his anguished warnings to a hurried planet, that his little girl, and her mommy, saw their last day on this ground made hallowed by the passing of their souls.

See how the shining purple ribbons wave in the wake of each passing car.

PROFILE

Two Springs

he wonders
will the telephone ever ring again
it has been a long quiet winter
with not enough work

bank accounts dwindle
wife needs grocery money
daughter a new sweater
mortgage electricity equipment loans payroll taxes
    insurances all must be paid

his workers need to earn income to support their
    own families
is the economy improving enough
will the telephone ring with clients this year

generations earlier a man sees his tribe's stored berries,
    nuts, dried meats and fish reduced then rationed
he stands on a knoll looking to the horizon hoping
    for signs that buffalo will return
will there be meat to nourish his people
or will the great spirit send the herds to other grazing
    grounds this year
will there be a desperate hunt fueled by hunger

he paces nervously
as the season of cold wanes

the days get noticeably longer
rain and warming soil awaken hibernating seeds
grass turns gray hills green
multiple days of sun and blue skies stir the earth
    from its long cold sleep

one man hears the telephone ring
the other thundering hooves in the distance

PROFILE

The Herd

A great herd of clouds, the color of enraged buffalo, thundered onto the Mendocino coast. They stampeded out light, turning all to black fear.

They mounted earth over and over, making hard love to her. Their potent semen impregnated her, bringing forth the birth of a million, million, million white seeds, coloring her otherwise gray skin a hope-filled, green.

Realizing that she was able to reproduce yet again, and ending her barrenness, earth took to the joy of motherhood, as if for the first time.

The Muse

Poetry barged through my door one day. There was no stealth in her movements, no cloak to hide her red hair, red lips and red attitude. She caressed, cuddled and had her way with me.

She came from the ocean during the red tide. I didn't beckon or invite her, she simply swept me away.

She came in Spanish and English and took my long words and whittled them to their core.

When in good humor, she gave herself without pause, or shame, and the verses flowed freely in meter and cadence as from a spigot. Other times she ripped a tooth from my jawbone in barter for a single line.

She had little patience with cowardice or hesitation and was a grand, jealous, and mischievous lover, often calling on me when I was long asleep, or slicing hot roast.

I began thinking that I understood her and could have my way with her. She jeered, and threw her head back and laughed when I wrote the false words she gave me as a tease.

PROFILE

So much do I want to understand her. I craved her friendship and devotion. She paused and looked at me for a moment, then spoke without color. "If you come to understand me, the magic will disappear," she warned. "I can only have spontaneous and lustful lovers. I have loved you as I have loved so many like you."

She smiled, lifted her blouse, and demanded that I tickle her pink nipple, then reached into her bag and put a peanut-sized phrase in my hand because she was in a generous mood.

The Pit

I know the fear of God, Satan, the world, and what it is to lose a childhood to the haunting fear of eternal damnation in the fiery pit of hell.

I know what it is to be ridiculed for having a different name, and feeling shame for being of my people.

I know what it is to be told, "You're not one of us, your skin is too light, you talk and dress like them, you're one of them."

I know what it is to lose even in victory.

I know how pent up fear and rage, express themselves through the tearing of one's own skin.

I know what it is to not trust the self, and the helpless feeling of being hired, realizing that a termination will soon come.

I know what it is to be the lesser of the males, and the pain of a broken back.

I know the dead eyes of life-term prisoners, the black whirlpool of drug addiction and its demonic dreams.

PROFILE

I know the jealousy and disdain of those who are joyous, and hate for those whom you are supposed to care for, and what it is to be deceived by someone you trust, and lie to someone you love.

I know what it is to slowly lose strength and the melting away of youth.

I know the dream of the drowned buck, with its magnificent antlers and its blank stare, as the final air bubbles emit from its splendid black nostrils.

I know what it is to desperately want to please, and to desperately love someone who will never love you.

I know the past and future of failure, what it is to hate the self, what it is to want to hide where no one can ever find you, and the temptation of wanting to sleep forever.

Where Are You?

Where are You when the torturer singes, rips, and breaks?

When the infant was pulled from the well, and breathed her last, did You care?

Are You saddened when a child starves, or when a cat toys with a mouse before tearing it to pieces? Or is it also sport for You?

Were You there when they told old man Contreras that his son hung himself in the jail cell? He tithed every week to Your house, even as his family was in need.

Were You there when the widower leaped from the bridge? Could You have not whispered *something* into his ear?

And where were You when she cast her children into the lake?

Can't You stop the little innocents from being fondled?

PROFILE

Come now, You could curl a finger and stop the burning tree from toppling onto the fawn.

Weren't You there when they found out Anne and her family and took them away?

Are You there when the emaciated, in the stench of their own urine, take a final drink?

Were You there when Lily wasted away? She died in agony as the disease spread. She was one of Your faithful servants, to the end. Was it necessary for her to suffer so much, or does it matter to You?

Where were You when He cried, "Why hast Thou forsaken Me?"

When our voices rise through the stained glassed windows of Your houses and land at Your feet, where are You?

POEMS

120/80

Her machine buzzes a warning. Its red digital numbers
blink on and off, 208/110, 208/110. My wife gasps and
removes the Velcro band wrapped around my arm.
"Maybe it's not so bad!" I say. "It's the silent killer," she
tells me, and makes an appointment with my doctor.
"Hmm," he says, "she's right, you know, pressure's much
too high. A perfect reading for you is 120/80. Take this
blue pill daily, but be advised, it may have a side effect.
Come back in two weeks." I don't miss a single day
taking the little blue pill that will make me perfect.

Two weeks later her machine's buzzer shrieks, red
numbers blink on and off 195/96, 195/96. "Still way too
high!" she says removing the band and dialing my doc.
"The pill's causing me to drool, doctor!" I say wiping
my chin. "Hmm," he says "don't worry, we'll get you to
120/80. You want to be perfect don't you? Add another
blue pill to bring it down a little and take this green one
to stop the flow. Come back in two weeks." "No-flow,"
reads the bottle's label. "Might have a side effect." I don't
miss a day taking two blue and one green pill that will
surely get me there.

I close my eyes and cross my fingers for good luck when
she straps on the machine. "180/96," she says then
reaches for the phone. I sit, grateful that at least the
damn buzzer's been silenced. "The No-flow is causing
me to hallucinate, doc. I've been hearing politicians

PROFILE

in my head giving speeches and they're telling the truth!" "Oh my!" says the doctor. "Oh my!" says the wife. "A pink one to supplement the blues and a yellow for the politicians, you're so close. It'd be a shame not to make it. See you in two weeks." Everyday it's two blue, a green, a pink, and a yellow that will make me perfect.

She straps on the machine and it reads, 143/84. She goes for the phone; I break down in tears. "The yellows have got me preaching from the Bible downtown on Sunday mornings, doc, and I'm getting a following!" "Here you are dear boy, a purple with red stripes for the preaching and this pretty turquoise with orange spots that'll finally get you to perfection, could have a slight side effect."

Doctor and wife stand quietly on the hillside overlooking the valley. Birds chirp in a tree, a breeze flutters the ribbon around the bouquet of flowers. The headstone reads: "Armando García-Dávila - A perfect 120/80: Cholesterol 400!"

Carry Me

The truth is I am tired of it. You know how it goes. One tires of the pace and of carrying this load of muscle and blood and bone. My toes bicker constantly with one another. My ankles and calves complain and whine. "This road of sixty-plus years is so much harder than it was. Where did the soft grasses and mud puddles you frequented go? And where are your mother's arms?"

My hands tire of tying shoelaces, shaving the same face, and brushing ever-thinning hair.

My eyes tire of reading angry newspapers and seeing the reflection of a progressively wrinkled face in the mirror each morning and of viewing inane television programs. Each eye has taken to a separate interest of late. While one adores gazing at flowers, the other leers at women. On Sunday last, one eye admired the red and white flowers in a planter box as the other gawked in the opposite direction at a pair of nicely filled nylons. Damn, it hurt and was terribly embarrassing walking into that telephone pole.

My soul is tired, tired of carrying so many loads of fear; the devil's sly craft at getting me to sin incurring God's eternal wrath, and the dread of phallic missiles that would incinerate the world in the batting of an eye. The thought of the earth sick with fever, her continents of ice fracturing and melting. It's a worrisome business!

PROFILE

I tire of doling out my earnings to men in suits: insurers, tax collectors, mortgage brokers. The mere sight of my checkbook brings me to uncontrolled weeping.

I tire of politicians and their organ-grinder masters, manipulating with promises of honey, while delivering bile.

I'm fed up with Christians who declare the remission of a disease of one of their own "a miracle from God," and children of other lands torn to bloody flesh by our bombs of war as nothing more than "collateral damage."

I've had it with "holy" men telling *me* whom I should hate. It would be delicious to stand in the middle of a packed fundamentalist service and scream out, "He died. He's not coming back. Get over it!"

The Greatest Poem

Soon I shall write the greatest poem ever written. I will be met at city gates and carried on the shoulders of cheering citizens to the town's square where mayors and councilmen will gather to hear me recite it.

The envy of every poet will run in green torrents down streets and into gutters. No anthology will be complete without *my* poem. Neruda, Whitman, Lorca, Borges, Homer, ha! Their names will all be listed after mine.

It won't be easy. I will reveal deep vulnerabilities causing men to cry and women to throw their fists in the air and shout, "You go, man!"

I will write of my convictions and philosophies, sparking new religions. Lamas and popes will give me their cell phone numbers.

I will never have to write a single verse again, living large off the royalties. Publishing houses will beg me to write more, anything! They will send me fat advances on works yet to be started.

I shall write the greatest poem ever written, right after dinner, or a refreshing nap. The muse will kneel at my feet massaging them as she nibbles on my ear whispering honey verses into it.

Brace yourselves because very soon, I shall write the greatest poem ever written.

PROFILE

You've Got Mail

It took a while before I finally gave in to buying the machine. "It will bring you the world," my grandchildren said. "But the world is too damn big to fit into this thing," I argued. "Haven't you heard of libraries where there are atlases? It's all the world you need!" "Whatever, grandpa," they said.

First it was learning how to turn it on. "Hold the button down," they said. "Don't let it go too quickly, hold it down a sec."

Then it was single clicking and double clicking using a rat. Like a fly caught in a spider web, I became more and more entangled in the web, in the electronic web, the World Wide Web.

A man's voice tells me, "You've got mail!" It's nice to hear people are sending me mail. I've never gotten all that much. But it turns out to be tasteless mail, there're no stamps or envelopes to lick, no taste at all! And I'm getting mail that I haven't asked for, but it isn't junk mail. Oh no, it's "spam," they tell me, but spam without eggs? Then it's not spam! "You've got mail," the man says every time I turn on the machine. He's starting to get annoying.

The machine gets sick now and then. It's always a virus and it takes a "geek doctor" who is summoned with the cure. He isn't half my age. Tap, tap, tap "that'll be $80," he says. "At least, my regular doctor takes my blood pressure and weighs me and gives me a bottle of sample pills," I tell the shaggy-haired geek doctor as I hand over my money. He doesn't even wear a smock to cover his tattered Levis.

"Whatever," he says rolling his eyes. "Whatever? Whatever? What's with this *whatever* crap?"

And now I've been set up with friends on the "Facebook," friends I didn't ask for or even remember having in the first place, and there are legions of them! I wish I could sit and have a beer with just one of my newfound friends. I complained about it to one of them. He "unfriended" me. Jerk.

There are cookies in the machine, but cookies without oatmeal or raisins? Then they're not cookies!

Now they're telling me that I should have a blackberry. I'd really like to have a blackberry, but just one? I'm told that these don't have juice to stain my fingers. "Then they're not goddamned blackberries!" "Whateverrr, Grandpa."

PROFILE

And there are people with a "My-Space," well what about the lady who would like to have *her* space or the poor bastard that would like *his* space or a group that might want their spaces? This my space guy sounds a little self-absorbed to me. He must be the same twit who tweets his twitter.

I'm not sold on this brand new world, not sold at all.

I turn on the machine. "You've got mail," the man says.

Go fuck yourself.

A Respite

There was tiredness in my love's eyes tonight.
But that I could have gently massaged her toes and feet,
her ankles and calves, her forehead, and flawless skin.

But that I could have disrobed her, covered her with a
quilt of down, kissed her weary hand, and let her drift
into a slumber to dream the romantic dreams of an
untroubled world.

PROFILE

Could You Love Me?

If I loved you? If, I, loved, you.

Could you love me?

Would you be here when the morning light greets the songs of the sparrows, or would I be left with a hundred cries, and your seed swimming in my belly?

If I would lay with you in the soft, supple grasses of spring, and satisfy your carnal desires, would you be here after our nap? And would you be able to love me without touching my hair, my breasts, or so much as my hand?

If I perfumed the straw of my bed for you, and painted my lips in scarlet, and rubbed your back, and danced naked for you, would you be willing to stroll next to me at the shore on a Sunday afternoon?

If I tickled you with my tongue when God sleeps, would you dance a lazy dance with me? Would you write verses and stanzas to my name?

If I anointed myself with oil and slithered with you under satin blankets, and made you feel like the red-plumed rooster, would you be here when the morning light greets the songs of the sparrows? Or would I be left with a hundred cries and your seed swimming in my belly?

Embers

The flames have subsided, and the heat has been absorbed in the walls. Glowing embers warm the house on this winter's eve.

It's no longer the passion of a new love, but her rubbing my sore back and neck after my day of labor. It's the soup she prepares for me and the glass of water she brings to take the dryness from my mouth in the middle of the night.

"Please be safe," she says when I leave each morning.

Walking through the park is our joy, and laughter the aphrodisiac.

The blaze of our love has subsided, the heartwood of oak, now embers, glow in the hearth warming our home from winter's chill.

PROFILE

An Exquisite Eve

Gently, I will knock on your door, when the heavens are clothed in sheer black silk. You will lie exquisitely naked by the flame of a candle.

Whispering, I will quietly love you in air sweetened by the flower of a jasmine, and we will sing the psalms of Eros.

Her Song

My melancholy, like a cold Irish fog, is centuries old, and saps life from my body and spirit. It turns children and puppies into nuisances and draws cynical amusement from the misfortunes of others.

Her song, whispered into my ear, is a beacon in this abysmal night of blue solitude. I hear its melody over the wail of the black wind. The power of her hymn is subtle yet steady, veering neither to the right or left, and warms from the stomach.

She gazes at the reflection of my fractured life in the shard of a broken mirror, seeing it whole.
Seeing, it whole.

She kisses my cold fingers and takes the green knives of self-deprecation and doubt from them, and puts them to sleep in their sheaves, then speaks the wondrous words of understanding. She lifts the cartload of guilt from my back, and dumps it into a deep ravine, where it is swept away by the white foam of tumultuous azure waters to the sea, for krill to devour.

"There is light," she assures. "Take my candlestick," she says. "But I can't see the handle," I reply. She laughs, then embraces me.

PROFILE

If I Loved You Yesterday

If I loved you yesterday, I love you more today.

If I loved you at dawn, then I love you all the more as the sun bids a good evening to the blue and green earth.

If I loved you when the hourglass was turned and one grain followed another, I loved you more with each falling particle, until the last nestled atop the mound.

If I loved you with this breath, then I loved you all the more with the next, and with each batting of an eye, and with each flutter of the hummingbird's wing, I loved you again and more.

I will heap my love for you after my day of labor, and sleep to dream of you, and then awake to love you more than the night before, because, my love, if I loved you yesterday, I love you more today.

Listen

Is it too much to ask?
Open a door for me.
Walk next to me.
Hug me once a day.

I will color my hair. I will paint my face to hide who I am, if it pleases you, just tell me that you love me once in a while. I'll hang those words on my wall, remembering that they passed through your lips.

And when the hour is late, before the lamp's flame has been snuffed, sit with me to tell me of your day.

And when the madness of the world spins like a black tornado, throwing me one side to another, hold your tongue, take my hand, then simply and quietly listen to me.

PROFILE

Of Little Boys and Kisses

Today my thoughts are the joyous thoughts of a little boy on a swing, for I know that she will be there to greet me on my return. I anticipate her smile wrapped around my tired eyes.

Hurry night, hurry day, break into a trot, pass quickly that the hour may soon arrive, that the smile and pocketful of kisses she has saved for me will not be in the distance, but here before my longing soul, that the minute may come that we shall embrace, that the second may come that our lips may lose their arid hours apart to be moistened by the kiss that says

"Hello my love, how I have missed you."

Of Love and Uncertainty

Uncertainty is all there is, my love.

Planets collide and explode in this chaotic universe. Gophers and beavers drown in their dens in this imperfect world. And one day there will be no day, for the earth shall cease its spinning.

We will take each other's hand, and walk this lonely trail together, each stone, each bend in the path a threat to our journey.

There are those who see us stumble. "Ha!" they say. "Did I not warn you of having faith in another?"

Fools we will be then, one to another, walking in light, wandering in shadows, for in the end my love, all that there is, is uncertainty and each other.

PROFILE

Loving Her

How I love her clean, soft flesh that smells of fresh cream on a Sunday morning.

How I love her tender breasts of jasmine that call to my mischievous fingers and tongue.

How I love her soft, moist crevasse playing a game of tag with my braggart rooster.

How I love her lying on me, lips to lips, navel to navel, toes to toes.

How I love the sweet breeze of her breath.

How I love her hair against the snowy pillow, like a mermaid's tiara around her radiant face that could surely launch a thousand ships.

Mi Leona

My love is a lioness, ripping her passions into my neck and shoulder. She is a thousand, thousand kisses, falling on me like hot rain. She is a hundred red explosions.

My love is an agitated ocean, pounding wave after wave, covering my jagged crags in her white foam, again and again, and then again, pitching her steam high into the air.

Her sensual fingers explore, and pinch, and rub, making love to my arms and chest and hair.

My love is Cupid's mischievous arrow, pricking me here, and there, and here again.

Naked, she is beauty and all things desirable, like the silver moons of August. Her shoulders are the whitest powdered snow, inviting *me*, to be the first to pass over them.

Our loving is angry and joyful and laughter and tears and delicious perspiration.

PROFILE

Regular Love

Hello my sweetheart. How was your day at work? I thought of you. I wondered and hoped that you were having a good day.

I love the days of the week with you: Tuesday, Wednesday, Thursday when you come home. I love the humdrum of the everyday, me writing at my desk, you taking a well-earned break laughing or crying with Oprah.

I love sitting with you having dinner and talking of nothing important. I love lying in bed with you, you with the remote in your hand catching the last of the news, me finishing a crossword puzzle. I love turning out the light, kissing you and saying, "Good night babe," then rolling over to feel your warmth under the covers and drifting off to sleep.

I love the regular.

Silence

It frightens me when you are silent.
It is as if you can see through me, as if I am made of glass, and my words stand naked before you with no place to hide.

It is disquieting when you don't speak.
It is as if the world has disappeared, as if time, light, shadows, the moon are no more, and the only things that I can be sure of are the darkness, and the cold, and loneliness.

Ah, *loneliness* who carried me in his back pocket for so long before I met you.

But just the same, I am frightened by your silence.
And your eyes, black as obsidian, are perfect mysteries revealing nothing to me, perfect mirrors, reflecting only what is before them:

a truth, a lie, a frightened child.

PROFILE

El Tango

La vida contigo es un tango. Life with you is a tango, sometimes tricky, sometimes sweaty, always bold, daring, grace, guts, and comedy!

You press your forehead to mine looking into my eyes, and stare into my soul, keeping me in time, in step, in tune.

My dance is slapstick, yours pure art. I, the clown, you, the ballerina. You take my hand in yours, put your arm on my shoulder and gently nudge, gently guide my clumsy self side to side to life's rhythms.

You whisper the cadences into my ear, "One, two, three, one, two, and one. Turn this way, now dip, hold me tight, tighter, like you mean it! Now turn."

They look on with envy, "They dance so well together." Ha! But that they only knew which is the dancer

Life with you is a tango, *la vida contigo es un tango, un tango fantastico!*

POEMS

A Winter's Alcove

There are sorrowful, chilled fogs these days that remind
one of his mortality. We are in that season when the
sun loses the eternal tug-of-war with the icy moon,
as exhausted leaves fall like wounded soldiers from
desperate trees.

It is the time when the earth falls into her hibernation,
to conceive the unhappy dreams of lost loves, a time
when we are reminded of whom we have offended, and
forgotten, and left behind. It is the time of cold rains and
hungry animals.

Let me kiss you, turn your collar up to the gray cold,
take your hand, and strut the joyous walk of love,
defying the face of the storm. I will create a warm alcove
for you in this river of iced waters, put my arms around
your sadness and for one brief and exotic moment take
you to where we will lie naked on warm blessed sands,
bask in the sun, and laugh at our melancholy.

Let us heap our fears in the cold night where they will
feel at home, polish our joys, and wear them around our
necks.

PROFILE

Wishing

How I wish that we didn't know each other's name, but only knew about one another through our eyes and lips and the yellow fruit that we like to eat.

How I wish that your hand was on my cheek, and that your aroma filled my room, and your smile was my nightlight.

How I wish that our pasts were erased, and that our hands had chalk to playfully script our futures in pinks and reds and crimsons.

How I wish I could put you on my bicycle and take you to the swings in the park.

How I wish you understood just how happy you make me, like a Sunday at the beach.

And how I like it when our souls chat like children anxiously waiting in line for ice cream.

Your Light

Who are you? From where does your light come?

Did you come on the wind from an Eastern winter, or did you emerge from a river of rose petals and chocolate?

Do you like the feel of sun-warmed soil under your toes, and soft cotton against your skin, or do you get your full-moon energy from blue silk at midnight?

It's been a happy dream chatting with your spirit. But I need to hear your laugh, touch your cheek, and hold your hand.

We must eat strawberries together while cooling our feet in a stream.

I want to wink and blush, steal a kiss, and contain shy laughter.

If I could hear the waves pound on the shore with you, and smell your hair. Perhaps then, I could understand from where your light comes.

"Yes!"

"Yes!"

Good God Almighty. She said, "Yes!"

I got on my knee and asked her, and she said, "Yes!"

My legs trembled, my voice quavered for the damned uncertainty, but she said, "Yes," with tears in her opened eyes she said, "Yes!"

I have so little to offer, but it seems to be enough for her that I am, simply who I am! "Quick, I better give her the ring so that she can't change her mind."

Will she continue to pat my cheek and laugh at my countless follies? Will she continue to smile every single day when she sees me?

"Oh crazy woman do you understand whom you are getting involved with?"

"Three immense Titans of ancient Greece could not hold the love that I have for you. Cupid has emptied his quiver into my hindquarters!"

Winter, summer, and autumn will be a springtime of joy each day. Daytime will provide the sun's light to see her face, and the night means sharing a bed, and sleep will bring the dreams of love and a world void of sadness.

I will give coins to beggars, candy to children, and smile at each stranger, because she said, "Yes, I will take this journey with you, yes, I will be your partner, yes, I will walk arm in arm, shoulder to shoulder with you."

Good God almighty. She said "Yes!"

PROFILE

American God

I was embarrassed being seen by beautiful Patricia with my family in our rattling station wagon on Sunday mornings. A Mexican Noah, my father. His ark of dents and worn tires filled with his creatures who had no choice in the matter.

Ma kept our clothes washed and pressed, but detergent and an iron could not mask faded shirts and pants worn through at the knees.

Other kids went to church in newer cars, with newer clothes, with newer parents.

We shared pews with Patricia and her family and the rest of the *Norte Americanos*. We all prayed in English, prayed in Latin, said the same orations, sang the same hymns.

But if we praised the same God in the same way, then why did He bless *them* so much more than us?

The *Campesinos'* Maestra

And it was in that season when the countryside is a painter's pallet of yellows and reds and crimsons that I met her.

She walked in a deliberate step even as *campesinos* in stained and soiled pants ran row to row slicing stems, stretched from the weight of bunches, sagging with the liquid sugar of the vines. Instinctively they found only the ripe.

Cut go.   Cut go.   Cut go.

But it was her wont to smile and speak with the certitude of a warm breeze, soft, gentile, quiet, but unquestioned resolve.

She had countless children under her charge loving each as her own, encouraging all to reach for the brass ring of life's carousel.

And the *campesinos*, who never knew such a teacher, continued their jog up and down row after row, parcel after parcel, acre after endless acre, making their wage kicking dust into the air, carried by the wind forming tunnels in the sky.

PROFILE

"Save them from this," beckoned the men in sweat and dirt and juice-soaked shirts.

She smiled, embraced their offspring. "I shall," she guaranteed, speaking with the measured conviction of the self-assured.

And the *campesinos*, they smiled the smile of hope and waved to *La Maestra* displaying like trophies their fingers, scarred and sliced and bandaged from the errant swing of the hook that divides stem from branch.

"I shall," she vowed, and walked off in a deliberate pace with her youthful charges in tow.

El Jardinero

I think of the *señora* in the morning, her legs, her arms; the sound of her laughter is the music of a silver harp guiding the lonely king to forgotten smiles.

Her hair is a field of gleaming wheat waving in a harvest breeze.

Señor Peacock fans his shining blue and green feathers and dances his luring dance for her, but alas in vain, for she would not settle for someone who offers only handsome plumage.

I think of her in the morning when the sun shines through her hair, aglow like a halo in the cool dawn. I hear her singing with the birds, serenading and welcoming the world from the land of happy and sad dreams. I think of her graceful walk, barefoot on rose petals, causing not so much as a bruise on those delicate wafers of the blossom.

I stole a glimpse of her silhouette through her gown; sun rays hugged, then passed around her gentle curves that would frustrate the most skilled sculptor.

PROFILE

I dream of touching, of embracing her, but what will she have of someone who is only hired to tend her garden? But that I could simply hold her smooth feet in my hands and wash them a hundred times, and when she naps, steal a kiss on each toe, on each heel, on each ankle, on each sole.

But that I could tell her of my love of her spirit. But that we could sit under the oak together, speaking only with our eyes.

This midday is hot, but I remember her in the cool morn, watering her garden and humming the hymn of the contented.

El Paletero

His fingers stop ringing the string of small brass bells
as he peddles harder pulling out of a lazy neighborhood
street and onto the avenue of honking horns and
screeching tires. Cars speed past this mobile vendor,
some a little too close for comfort drawing concerned or
vexed glances from harried drivers.

He offers *paletas*: frozen fruit bars of coconut, strawberry,
tamarind, watermelon. Can he earn enough today selling
popsicles to feed his family? His shirt is dark with sweat,
but one must do what one must to meet his obligations;
si no trabajes no comes (if you don't work, you don't eat).

A sparrow living this adage pulls a worm from an area
where cats are known to dwell – a risky business indeed.
He flies up into a tree and eyes the man peddling the
insulated box on bicycle wheels passing below him.

El Paletero slows his pace as he rides into another
neighborhood and begins working his bells like a
maestro hoping to lure those with a sweet tooth and a
little extra to spend.

The sparrow bounces branch to branch until he is at
his nest and puts bits of today's earnings into anxious
little beaks as children line up at the curb hopping with
excitement clutching coins in their little hands.

PROFILE

El Gran Viento

A great wind blows from the south to the north.

A great wind blows, from the south, to the north, over mountain and valley, over desert and river, and under and over and through the hands of those who would try to stop it.

A great blowing wind a thousand miles long, bringing with it a language and a food, an accordion and a fiddle, and a song for each star in the heavens.

A great wind blows from the south to the north bringing hope and determination; the hope of a home, and the determination to earn it.

Coyote and hawk know this wind. Armadillo and antlered buck, rattlesnake, puma; and the ancient peoples of this land recognize this wind that blows from the south to the north.

They say.

"It is the grandchild of the cold wind that blew across the great waters that have no end. The wind, which brought a thousand huge canoes with sails."

They say.

"It is the cousin of the wind that blew from the east to the west bringing people in wagons covered with cloth; people with a curious tongue and the curious songs of the accordion and the fiddle."

"Ah," they say, "this fickle wind will change its course one day, and then blow from the north to the south."

PROFILE

Monks of the Field

Now, cool, quiet, serene. Hills the green of Ireland.
Clear as glass, this February air.
And sun, glorious sun, against a sky so deep, so blue,
one forgets it has ever rained.

Faint sounds from the distant valley below:
a car engine on a road somewhere,
the caws of crows echo overhead.
A single engine airplane putters along an endless
horizon.

Snip, snap, clip-clip, snap, the rhythm of pruning shears
in the strong and calloused hands of field workers. A
laborer, the hood of his sweatshirt pulled over his head,
examines the dormant vine as if it is the only vine on
earth.

"Field workers," "farm workers," *"campesinos,"* from
Oaxaca, from Guanajuato, Michoacán, a hundred places
that one hears of. But monks they are, monks of the field,
observing an unspoken oath of silence, observing an
ancient and holy motto: *"laborare orare est"*— "to work
is to pray."

Each man living, working in the moment, in the second,
no tomorrow for him, no yesterday, no morning, or
evening; only the ever present now.

Sixty-five acres—50,000 vines to prune over these hills and valley. Are there too many for this crew of Alejandro, Noè, Manuel, Crisando, and Gabriel? Only one vine in the here, in the now, for each silent man.

By-and-by each vine will be pruned and retied to the stake, to the galvanized wire. By-and-by all pruned branches tossed between the narrow rows will be disked and tilled into the vineyard to become soil. By-and-by each vine will be sulfured in spring, thinned in summer, its purple fruit gathered in a frantic fall harvest when the sugar content is exact.

But in this now, there is only an infinite blue heaven, and silent monks of the field, their pruning shears chattering in the silence.

PROFILE

El Otro Lado

He stands at the river's edge. Wisps of clouds turn red in the coming dawn. Some flying insects escape the jaws of largemouth fish in the hovering mist. To his back the motherland with sad breasts deplete of milk. To his back his woman and offspring. Ah, but to his front the land of a foreign tongue and foreign ways, peopled with those who will hate or pity him. To his front, a chance to prove himself, a chance to provide for those dependent on his muscle and dreams. To his front, mountains of work in *El Norte* where there is labor for a million strong men.

On ranches, one must stoop and strain and lug and bend, and there are countless herds of sheep, and cattle, and horses to tend. There is work in factories, estates, kitchens, and in the fields, work pouring cement, driving nails, planting trees, and serving meals, there is labor by day, labor by night, labor on the day of rest, putting the stamina of legs, backs, and arms to the test. There is never ending work in orchard and in vineyard from horizon to endless horizon.

And the river, the great dividing river flows slowly, calmly, deliberately, as if no one has ever drowned while being pursued through its currents in the angry season of tumultuous waters, as if there were never a time of a ravenous torrent with an insatiable appetite that consumes all things from the docile cow to the venomous viper, and any other man or beast or flower or tree that dares it.

The river, the river burdened with the task of dividing avarice-plagued nations. But on this day, and in this dawn, this river that perpetually moves from the yesterday to the tomorrow, and yet is perpetually in the here, seduces this man, lures him to ford its waters, invites him to look into his future.

He gazes into a pool to see not a man in tattered pants and a worn out sombrero, but the reflection of a *caballero*. A gentleman, a man of means who stands straight and pays his own way, and on Sundays takes his family to church in an automobile.

There, reflected in the baptismal water is a man in fine clothes, with hair that is combed and trimmed regularly.

This is what the big river offers, and it is all his to seize, if he simply crosses to *El otro lado* undetected by those who would keep him from his destiny.

PROFILE

Fresas

One straight furrow follows another and another along a landscape that looks as if a colossal comb was run over it.

Ignacio spent most of his life preparing, planting, and harvesting this acreage.

His knees ache with rheumatism. "He spent too much time in the cold damp earth," Doña Flor, his wife says.

Strawberry shortcake, strawberry jam, strawberry ice cream; and see how lovely they look on the cereal box, deep red against white milk and flakes of grain; food for happy, healthy people.

Ignacio built a house in his native land after working and saving for most of 30 years in these fields. His house is solid: constructed of lumber, blocks, mortar, and wiring for electricity and plumbing for running water.

It is time to plant vegetables in his garden but his swollen joints do not allow him to do so, at least not today. Maybe tomorrow his body will feel up to it, and besides his son, Alejandro, leaves for *"El Norte"* today. The season for preparing the soil for planting strawberries has come.

Unknowingly, many will toast the labor of these men when they enjoy ice-cold strawberry daiquiris on warm summer afternoons.

POEMS

Which Foot?

My hands harvest fruit from tree and vine in this land of promise. I labor as an angry sun causes me to sweat rivers. I perform any job willingly: wash floors, remove the innards of butchered hens, construct homes so that the citizens of this nation may live in comfort.

Calloused hands I trade for a wage, for my children to have a chance. I live in the most modest of homes without complaint, only grateful for the opportunity of employment.

But my feet shall remain firmly planted in the land of the eagle and serpent. One day I will return to the town of my birth in a shining new vehicle. I will stroll the plaza each evening dressed in store-bought clothes. "*Hizo bien, hizo bien*, he did well!" they will whisper. "He worked decades and has returned to build his family a house!"

But alas, my children's feet are taking root here! I talk to them in our tongue; they answer me in this other! "Ju noh leeve heer," I tell them in this foreign language. They only hide their smiles and laugh.

PROFILE

"*No somos de estos*, we are not of these people!" I remind them. "Here we only inhabit a house; our home, our hearts are over there; there can be no other way! Here we stoop; there we stand."

"Ask *Papá*, are there hamburgers in this land of yours?" My children also ask, "Are there games to play on screens that flash green and white and red?"

One foot supports my body; one foot supports my soul; on which foot do I stand?

Wild Flowers

They don't grow in greenhouses, nurseries, or tended gardens, and survive on but a single season of rain. Borne of hardship they are tempered and thrive where the less hardy wither away.

The wildflower seed migrates riding the wind, the wind that recognizes no borders. When in foul moods, the wind casts the seed onto barren rock or wetlands, fated to dry under a merciless sun or sink into the mire. When in good humor, the wind sets the seed onto arable land to germinate and rise tall and firm, but even here it may be consumed by grazing herds.

The migrant rides this angry or gentle wind to the land of opportunity. He makes his perilous odyssey leaving the barren ground of the homeland where his aspirations have long since been scattered by the arid storms of greed. He comes seeking those grueling labors that the less hardy are unable to do.

Desperate for a chance to sprout and grow, he pays smugglers to slip him into the land of eternal promise, but at times he is abandoned, and left to the fate of the wildflower drying in the desert under an unforgiving sun. At times he is swept away while attempting to cross the river of hope. And even when he succeeds at crossing, he often falls victim to the avarice of godless bosses.

PROFILE

But fueled by the dreams of earning a dignified life, he continues his arduous treks on, and on, and on. And the forever wind carries countless seeds of wildflowers to uncertain destinations, casting them onto barren rock or sowing them over fertile loam.

Behold, how their blossoms in every color grace the land.

STORIES

Bless Me Father for I Have Sinned

MY TWIN, FERNANDO AND I walked slowly down the aisle, each with his girl partner toward the altar to receive communion. We wore white shirts, black shoes, and the new navy blue slacks that our parents had tailor made in Tijuana, just south of where we lived in San Diego, California. The pants had pressed cuffs, creases, and were stylishly loose-fitting. Our older siblings never got such lavish items as tailored clothes. Pa's truck-driving salary didn't allow for such extravagances, but Ferd and I were Ma's little twin dolls.

The girls wore white lacy dresses, veils, and patent leather shoes. We all carried prayer books draped with rosaries and had been sitting in the pews, as still as second graders were able. When the time came to receive communion, we rose, formed couples, and slowly walked to the front of the church to kneel at the communion rail. I had seen my family and the bigger kids of my Catholic grammar school receive this blessed sacrament all of my life. At long last, this was *my* First Holy Communion.

In order to receive the body of Christ, we had to fast from all foods and drink, even water, since the night before. I felt light headed and my stomach growled like an angry cat. Father McGuinn walked along the communion rail, placing the sacred hosts on the new communicants tongues. An altar boy followed Father, holding a shiny brass paten under our chins to catch whatever minute scraps of the consecrated host that would otherwise fall to the floor and become desecrated. We were told to never

ever touch the sacred host, but to swallow it immediately. Only a priest's consecrated hands were allowed to touch the shiny little wafer of unleavened bread that was now Jesus Christ.

The nuns did a fine job of preparing us for this profound moment in our religious lives. They taught us of the sacraments; baptism had cleansed our souls of Adam and Eve's "Original Sin." They disobeyed God by eating of the forbidden fruit in the Garden of Eden. Disobeying one's parents was one thing. But how could anyone even consider disobeying Almighty God? Anyhow, we had inherited their sin and we couldn't enter heaven until it was cleansed by the holy water of baptism.

Baptism was a ritual performed by an ordained priest. But when someone who wasn't baptized was hurt in a car accident or wounded on a battlefield and they were dying, then anyone could baptize them by pouring holy water over their head while saying, "I baptize thee in the name of the Father, and of the Son, and of the Holy Ghost." Regular water would do if there wasn't holy water near by. I asked during a religion class, "What if the person has only seconds to live, and the water is far away? Could I use spit?" Sister didn't answer.

I worried about my little neighbor, Chris. He was a first grade public school kid whose family wasn't Catholic and never went to church. I didn't want him to miss out on going to heaven with me. I took him into the garage one afternoon and explained Baptism to him. I then poured water over his head and said the holy words. I felt great. I was in the second grade and had already saved my first soul.

STORIES

Holy Eucharist (consuming the body of Christ) was the next sacrament. Sister Alvira Marie, our second grade teacher, told us that before receiving Holy Communion our souls had to be cleansed from the splotches of sin and be "white as a bottle of milk." She then told us the story of a girl who didn't confess a big sin, and when she went to communion, "the host singed her tongue!" I imagined the girl screaming and running from the church as steaming saliva billowed from her mouth.

Confession, the forgiveness of sins, was the next sacrament. Small sins were "venial," big ones "mortal." The punishment for a mortal sin was to be sent to hell and burn forever. Kids rarely committed mortal sins like murder, although I really wanted to kill my little sister, Carmen.

"No!" said Sister, answering another of my hypothetical questions during class, "If a person killed somebody by accident God wouldn't punish them, but He would know if they did it intentionally. Then he would punish them." So, I thought, if I killed my little sister and made it look like an accident, then the police would let me go and I wouldn't get the electric chair, but God would send me to hell. I could just see the little brat looking down at me and getting the last laugh. But if it really was an accident that only looked suspicious, then I'd get the chair, but go to heaven. What if she could be gotten rid of and it really *was* an accident? Then I wouldn't get it from anyone. I prayed for divine intervention.

There was a cold and heavy fog outdoors last Friday when we walked into the church to make our first confession. I was in mental anguish. Surely Father would recognize my voice and know that it was me who would

PROFILE

confess to looking at one of my older sisters once when she was changing her clothes. Sins of the flesh were among the worst a person could commit. But if I didn't tell him of this great sin, then it wouldn't be forgiven, and I would receive Holy Communion with a mortal sin on my soul and I'd wind up in hell forever.

There were three doors in the wall: door number one, door number two, and door number three. Father waited for us behind door number two ready to hear of our sins. Sister lined a few of us on either side of the confessional and sat the rest in pews to "examine our consciences" while we waited our turns. She opened door number one and pushed in the first little sinner, Ruth, and did the same at door three, making my friend Gerry go in. In a few minutes Ruth came out, walked to the front of the church, and knelt to say her penance prayers. Sister signaled the next little lamb to take her place. Door number three opened. Gerry stepped out and walked down the aisle to join Ruth in the penance pew. And the holy carwash began. Dirty little splotched souls entered, and shiny clean ones exited.

I knelt in the pew sweating it out. Father was about to learn that I was a lecher of the worst sort. How could I possibly convince him that I really wasn't, but a good Catholic boy who would like to be a saint someday? I hoped that there would be an earthquake or maybe Father would have a heart attack before I had to go in, but no luck. It was my turn. I hesitated to enter the confessional. Sister glared at me.

I hung my head, opened the door, and walked in. It was dark in the small cubicle. I knelt on the pad in front of the little screen in the wall. I heard mumbling; some kid on the other side was confessing. Hey, what if his sins were really big so mine wouldn't seem so bad. What if he murdered someone? There was a brief silence and then the little door across the screen slid open. I could see Father's silhouette against the wall behind him. My anxiousness erased months of preparation, and I forgot how to start my confession.

Father waited a bit then asked, "Are you here to confess?"

"Um, yes Father."

"You may start."

"I forgot how."

"Bless me Father..."

"Oh, yeah! Bless me Father for I have sinned. This is my first confession. Since I was born I've fought with my brothers and sisters a whole, whole bunch of times. If I told you a hundred but it was really a hundred and one, then could I go to hell for missing that one?" Father put his fist to his mouth and coughed to hide a chuckle.

"Just do the best you can, my son."

"And I disobeyed my parents a whole lot of times too. I wish I could tell you how many, um, maybe about a thousand?" More coughing.

Quick! Make up some sins, so I won't have to tell him the whopper! "And, and Father. I, I threw rocks at the neighbor's cat, but my mom told me to because it kept pooping in her garden. And once after I saw Moe poke Curly Joe in the eyes, I did it to my little sister and made her cry! And, and um..." I was in a tug-of-war, too ashamed to tell this holy man of my terrible sin, but if I didn't, then Jesus would host a barbeque in my mouth. There was no escape.

PROFILE

My voice broke with emotion. "And, and Father I, I committed a real nasty sin." He leaned toward me.

"Yes, my son, tell me about it."

"Father I, I tried to look at one of my sisters when she was changing her clothes." I started to cry in humiliation and expected his fist to smash through the screen and smack me in the face, but he only sat silently for a moment.

"I see. Well, did you see anything?"

"No, Father. She knew I was in my bed and kept looking at me. I couldn't get the covers high enough to get a good look. I saw something that looked like my uncle's bald head; must've been her butt."

Father went into a coughing fit. I felt bad about making him so sick. He settled down.

"Well, God is proud of you for having had the fortitude to confess this, but you must understand that this is an invasion of privacy. Wouldn't you be embarrassed if people looked at you when you were dressing?"

"Yes, Father. I'll never ever do it again."

"Very good. For your penance say three Hail Mary's and three Our Fathers. Now say the Act of Contrition."

"Oh, my God, I am heartily sorry for having offended thee, and I detest my sins because of thy just punishments…" As I prayed, he recited the forgiveness prayer and ended by raising his hand and making the sign of the cross.

"I absolve thee in the name of the Father, and of the Son, and of the Holy Ghost. Amen. Go and sin no more. You're a good and brave boy."

"Gee, thanks Father!"

I was absolved of my sins! I felt like skipping all the way down the aisle to the penance pew. The sun broke through the fog outdoors and shone through the stained glass windows, brilliantly lighting up the church. My soul, after saying my penance prayers, was white as a bottle of milk. What a feeling! I could be killed on the way home and go straight to heaven!

All I had to do was stay sin free at least until my first communion on Sunday. I'd have to obey my parents, not fight with my siblings, or sneak into my sister's bed to scare the hell out of her at night. I had barely managed to stay clean over the weekend except for when I flicked a booger at Carmen, but I missed so it probably wasn't a sin.

Sunday had finally come. I walked with my partner to the communion rail. Father McGuinn stopped in front of me. He put a hand into the golden chalice and took out a host. I closed my eyes, raised my head, and stuck out my tongue. The alter boy put the paten under my chin.

"Corpus Cristi," Father said placing Jesus on my tongue. I tried to swallow him as taught, but couldn't! He was stiff as cardboard, and my mouth was dry and pasty from not eating or drinking since dinner last night. I tried again and gagged, nearly coughing Him out onto the floor. Mercifully, Jesus finally softened to mush and slid down. I walked back to the pew.

It was done. Jesus was in me, but I didn't feel any different than I did before! I looked at my partner to see if she looked different somehow. She didn't. I caught my twin's eye and whispered over his partner sitting between us. "Feel anything?" He shrugged his shoulders. I gave him a "what the heck?" look. Sister, sitting behind me pinched my shoulder. I turned, closed my eyes, and lowered my head pretending to pray. Maybe there was some-

PROFILE

thing deep inside that I had to think about in order to feel Jesus' presence. I kept trying but nothing came.

Toward the end of mass I felt something on the roof of my mouth. I put my finger to it and drew out a small glob of a curious looking white paste. I stared at it for a second before the revelation came. IT'S JESUS! I shot my finger back in my mouth and swallowed His arm, or leg, or whatever body part. Holy smokes! Was this a sin? Did I need to confess it? I prayed my mouth wouldn't start burning.

Mass seemed to go on forever before we finally got to walk down the aisle with our partners, parading past our families, out of the church. Ma had Pa take a picture of my twin and me standing at the church wall in our new shirts and tailor-made pants.

From that day forward, on the first Friday of each month, we got to join the third through eighth graders to receive communion at mass before school. I got one of those cool cinnamon rolls and cartons of milk at my desk for breakfast just like the rest of the big kids. Boy, in the name of the Father, and of the Son, and of the Holy Ghost, this was great!

Don't Fall Asleep

WE HAD JUST SEEN *THE WOLF MAN* and I was lying in the dark with my twin brother, Ferd, and our sisters, Ana, Carolyn, and Martha. We were in the living room lying on olive-green army surplus cotton-stuffed mats. Ana and Carolyn were the oldest and in high school. They had allowed Ferd and me to stay up with them, and Martha who was in sixth grade, to watch the Friday night scary movie on TV. Ferd and I had been so excited! We got to stay up late, eat popcorn, drink soda, and watch a movie that didn't even start until 9:00 o'clock.

It was terribly dark and quiet after we turned in. I looked around the room and into the kitchen. There he was. I could see the Wolf Man's silhouette, lit by the faint moonlight. He was waiting for me to fall asleep before making his move to get me. He had been attacked and bitten by a wolf and was cursed to become a Wolf Man. I saw him turn into the monster that was half wolf and half man. He didn't want to be one, but that was the curse; on a full moon, the hair on his face and arms and legs grew longer and longer, and his teeth got big and sharp. He walked through the fog and found his first victim, a poor old man happily smoking his pipe and raking leaves. The old guy didn't stand a chance against the powerful Wolf Man.

Carolyn's back was to me. I scooted closer and turned, putting my back against hers. She was hot, but I was hotter, especially with the blankets over me. Even so I kept my

PROFILE

back, butt, and legs up against her.

She shifted half-asleep, "Back off," she said.

"I'm scared," I whispered. "I think he's in the kitchen."

"Who?"

"The Wolf Man."

"No he's not, *cuatito*. There's no such thing, now go to sleep," she said as she reached back and patted my hip. She pulled away. I heard deep breathing coming from my other sisters. They were lucky to be sleeping. I wished I could. I peered out from under my blankets. He was still in there. And he wasn't happy about my telling on him. I wanted to say I was sorry, but it'd only make things worse for me.

I broke out in a sweat and wanted to pull off the covers, but moving around might trigger his attack all the sooner. And me being exposed, he'd be able to tear straight into my skin. At least the covers protected me a little. My only hope was to scream when he came for me, then Carolyn would yank me back from him and we'd all fight him off until Pa came running down the hall to save us. No one was stronger or braver than our Pa.

I looked toward the kitchen. *Hijo!* He had sneaked behind the door and was peeking at me through the crack between the door and hinges. I had to do something. I tapped my sister's back. "Carolyn," I whispered, "Carolyn."

"Ayyy, what do you want?"

"Can I sleep between you and Ana?"

"I don't care, just settle down!"

I sprang to my knees and rolled over her, dragging my blanket with me, and landed between the two.

"Ayyy, what are you doing?" Ana said.

"Nothing," I said softly, covering myself with the blanket. I was safe at last. But it didn't take but a minute to realize that it was much hotter between my sisters. At least I couldn't see over their bodies into the kitchen. I lay quietly sweating and listening for the Wolf Man to come around from behind the door.

Somebody shuffling blankets broke the silence. Then I heard Ferd whisper, "Martha, Martha."

"Whaat?!"

"I'm scared."

"Go to sleep! I told you, Carolyn. We shouldn't have let them see the stupid movie!"

My good luck; Ferd and Martha had drawn the Wolf Man's attention away from me.

I felt something against my cheek and put my hand to it. It was a piece of popcorn. I stealthily picked it up and sneaked it into my mouth. I didn't dare chew it. The crunching would draw the Wolf Man's attention back to me. The popcorn had salt and butter and tasted good. It slowly dissolved in my mouth, and I slowly dissolved into sleep.

PROFILE

Chato's Steal

In spring, Christ and baseball are risen. I never understood the importance of this hallowed sport until the day that my father voluntarily came out of the house and squatted like an umpire to call balls and strikes for my twin brother and me. We had signed up for Saint Rita's Grammar School baseball team and were practicing for tryouts. My father! The same man who never did much more than smoke cigarettes and drink beer when he wasn't eating, watching sports on television, or sleeping before working the graveyard shift at the trucking company from midnight to eight in the morning delivering freight. But he gave up his precious free time to coach us on playing baseball.

We made the team and got real uniforms. I put mine on and gazed at myself in the mirror. I looked just like a major leaguer! Pa drove us to practices and never missed a game. It became a part of our routine, like going to church on Sundays, except that Ma and my sisters weren't involved. They only heard about our coaches and teammates, and descriptions of the games that we always seemed to lose.

"It's only a game," Martha, one of my older sisters, said. But what did she know about competition?

"Duck when a pitch is close. It can make an inside strike look like a ball," Pa yelled from the pitcher's mound he constructed in the backyard. "Ready? Here it comes. Oh jeeze, you're 'stepping in the bucket. You're backing away because you're afraid of getting hit by the ball. Don't be afraid. Stand closer to the plate and swing, *Chato.*" Chato. I hated that name. It was a Spanish term referencing a person's nose. I fell and broke it when I was little, and it remained a bit disfigured.

"It's okay to have that name," Pa explained. "In Mexico people call each other names like that all the time and think nothing of it. There was a man with one leg when I was kid in Mazatlán. Know what everybody called him?" Ferd and I shrugged our shoulders. "*Mocho*, Stump!" Ferd and I snickered.

"And I knew a man who had to have one of his balls cut off because it had cancer. We called him '*huevo*,' egg!" Ferd and I busted out laughing. "The gringos are ready to fight you if you find something unusual about them and then give 'em a nickname around it. Mexicans don't get mad. It's your street name and makes you one of the guys."

"I wasn't born in Mexico," I told Ferd when we lay in our bunk beds that night. "I still hate being called Chato." Pa called Ferd *"El Aguzado,"* the smart one. Ferd, a little bigger and stronger than me, outdid me at most everything: wrestling, running, even school work. But at baseball we were close to equals.

This was our team's rookie season, and it showed. Our coaches couldn't keep us from fooling around at practices. And once our manager, Mr. Rodriquez, was warming us up before a game by hitting ground balls to the infielders. He smacked a smoker to his son, Cruz, who was playing second base. The ball took a bad hop and hit him in the mouth. Cruz wailed as his father carried him off the field. We found chunks of his teeth lying on the ground by his position. He came to our next practice with a set of gleaming silver front teeth that reflected the sun.

PROFILE

We lost one game after another. I was bored in left field once and started making designs in the dirt with my cleats. I heard people screaming as the ball sped between my feet. I ran to the fence, picked it up, and threw it hard to the infielders. The batter got a triple and cleared the bases. If I'd been on my toes, he'd gotten a single and only one man would've scored.

"What the hell were you doing out there, Chato?" Pa said on our drive home. "You weren't paying attention to the damn game!" I sat quietly in the car looking down at the floor. "Not paying attention." It's what my teachers were always telling me.

We became the "doormats" of the league. St. Didicus got the best of us. St. Agnes pounded us. St. Anthony's gave us a holy beating, scoring 13 runs to our 3. Our coach, Mr. Aguilar, sat us in the dugout after that one.

"You guys couldn't beat a troop of girl scouts! You're playing like dead men out there! It's a goddamn embarrassment!"

Word got around the parish of his outburst and Monsignor Gallagher, the pastor, had a talk with Mr. Aguilar. "Now, Ramon, you mustn't set a bad example for these lads just because you've lost a few games."

Our team rose from the dead for one glorious moment. It was the final game of the season. Pa sat on the slope overlooking the field, where he got a better view than did the people who sat in the bleachers below. We went into the bottom of the last inning actually tied at three runs with Saint Jude's. There were two outs when I got my ups. I worked the count full, three balls and two strikes. The next pitch barely caught the inside of the plate, but I ducked away and fooled the umpire.

"Ball four!" he yelled. "Take your base batter." It should've been strike three and the end of the game. I jogged to first hiding my smile. I didn't dare let their pitcher, Frankie Santana, see me. I could feel his scowl. I was afraid of him. He was big for his age and was always picking on kids smaller than him. He threw rocks at me once on my way home from school. All I could do was run scared.

Pete Piedras, my closest friend on the team, came up next. He was our best player. He could hit, catch fly balls, snag grounders, and throw hard with accuracy. He hit a single and advanced me to second. Then scrawny little Felipe, whom we called *Perrito*, came to bat. It was a given that he'd be the final out of the game. He reached base only three times all year, and two of those came by way of throwing errors. Perrito was a bonafide "strikeout King." Everyone knew it including Frankie, who fired his first pitch over the plate.

"S-t-e-e-r-i-k-e one," the umpire yelled raising his arm. I stole third base and didn't even draw a throw from the catcher, Eddie. Eddie was one of Frankie's cronies.

Eddie wasn't paying attention to me and threw the ball back to Frankie. The strategy was obvious: "strike out the little *pendejo*." Frankie sneered and aimed his next pitch, a screaming fastball, right at Perrito. Perrito flung out of the batter's box and fell to the ground. His batting helmet went tumbling up the third base line.

"Back in the batter's box, son," the umpire said. Frankie's plan worked. Perrito got back into the box but stood as far away from home plate as possible, leaving it a wide-open target. He raised his bat into the air, trembling with fear.

PROFILE

Coach curled his fingers through the chain-link fencing of the dugout. He looked at the ground and shifted the dirt with his toe, waiting for the inevitable end of a miserable season for a bunch of rookies. The best he could hope for was to tie one lousy game.

I took a long lead from third and could have easily been thrown out, but Frankie threw the ball hard to the plate. Dust exploded from the catcher's mitt.

"S-t-e-e-r-i-k-e two!"

"Frankie's going in for the kill," I thought. Then it hit me. No one was paying attention to me. What if I tried stealing home? The catcher smiled wickedly as he brought his arm forward throwing the ball to Frankie for the final strike. *Now! Now! Now!* screamed a voice in my head. I broke for home. By the time Eddie noticed me it was too late; the ball was out of his hand and on its way to Frankie. Eddie jumped to his feet and landed between home plate and me. I slid feet first with my eyes closed. Eddie stretched his mitt high over his head reaching for Frankie's frantic throw. My cleats collided with Eddie's. His body flew sideways and landed on mine. The momentum took us both sliding over the plate. Everyone sprang to their feet, craning their necks witnessing the collision at home.

Did he catch the ball? Was I out? I opened my eyes to see through a cloud of dust the umpire bent over with his arms outstretched like a bird on the wing.

"S-a-a-a-f-e!"

Safe? Safe? I was raised from the earth as coach set me on his shoulder. Screams and cheers filled the air. He put me down to the back-slapping and head-slapping and shoving of my teammates. Frankie slammed his mitt to the ground. His lower lip quavered in anger and frustration.

I looked at him and narrowed my eyes. "I got you, *carbon*," I said softly.

Pa laughed and patted me on the knee several times on the drive home. "That was heads up ball, *Mijo*. That was heads up ball." He stopped at a liquor store for a can of ale and bought Ferd and me candy bars.

Later that afternoon I was sitting on the back porch with my little neighbor, Chris. I dropped my pants, showed him the large red burn on my hip from the slide home.

"It's what baseball players call a 'strawberry,'" I said proudly.

I heard Pa talking excitedly to Ma and my aunt and uncle in the house.

"And then he made for home and slid over the plate, and ha, ha, ha, he knocked the ball out of the catcher's mitt! And Armando won the game! Our Armando won the game!"

PROFILE

Voice Behind the Wall

My older brother, Tony, took me to meet a woman who lived behind a wall. He drove me after my Little League baseball practice to a neighborhood where hardly any houses needed painting and the lawns were green and mowed, the shrubs neatly trimmed.

"She lives up there," Tony said, pointing to the top of a hill where an old three-story house stood. It had long green fingers of ivy crawling up its walls and huge trees that kept it in shade. It reminded me of a house I'd seen in a Dracula movie.

"What does she do?" I asked.

"You'll see," he said, looking over his shoulder at me as we scaled the concrete stairs leading to the house.

"Will I be able to see her?" I asked, panting a little as we climbed the steps.

"No."

"Can't I just go back down and wait for you in the car?"

"No! Now keep going!"

I, like my Ma, Pa, and the rest of the family, had complete faith in Tony. He was in his fourth year studying to be a priest at Immaculate Heart Seminary in San Diego where we lived, but this time he was stretching the limits of my trust. Why would he think that I'd want to meet some strange woman who lived behind a wall? And what if she had a way of snatching kids?

"Will I be able to see her?"

"No, I told you! Now don't be afraid."

When we reached the porch, Tony grabbed the worn brass knocker and banged it against the door. I tried to take his hand, but he brushed mine away. I could hear faint shuffling inside as someone neared. The doorknob turned. The door opened with a creak. A thin, wrinkled woman dressed in a black nun's habit peered at us through a set of thick wire-rimmed glasses. She nodded at Tony, then with her bony finger, signaled us in. I followed Tony inside.

It took a moment for my eyes to adjust to the dimness in the entry hall. The old woman closed the door behind us. It echoed through the cavernous room.

"Sister Theresa," Tony said.

The old woman nodded, then walked across the room and disappeared out a door on the opposite side.

I noticed a wooden cylinder the size of a small barrel that was constructed into the wall. Tony pointed to a chair by the cylinder. "Sit there," he said.

The room smelled musty, reminding me of the time my twin and I had crawled under our house, and everything, even the dirt, smelled old.

The wooden benches, chairs, and a tall chest of drawers gleamed. On the walls down the darkened hallway were rows of painted portraits of saints. It was still and calm like the sanctuary of my church, where I served Mass as an altar boy during the sunrise service.

I had brought my mitt with me and pressed it with both hands against my chest. It was the only thing that offered a sense of familiarity and comfort. The glove still had a new reddish-tan look, though I had used it all season and it was close to being broken in. I heard something move behind the wall next to me and pulled away.

PROFILE

"Sister Theresa?" Tony said.

What in the heck is he doing? I wondered. *This is getting weird.*

"Hello!" said a woman's voice. "How are you, Antonio?"

Holy smokes, there's a woman trapped behind the wall!

"Doing fine, Sister. I know it's close to time for your midafternoon prayers. I thought I'd stop by for a quick visit."

He's talking to a nun who's stuck behind the wall! I remembered a woman who had screamed at me when I hit a baseball through her window last year. I never saw her face, though she must have been ugly from the way her deep and raspy voice sounded. Maybe this nun was ugly and didn't want anybody to see her.

"Who have you and the sisters been praying for lately?" Tony said.

"The early morning Matin session was dedicated to death row prisoners and single mothers, the midmorning Prime was offered for the mentally ill and their families. The Laud will be devoted to peace in the Middle East, and we get so many prayer requests from people who drop in with personal petitions. One poor soul asked us to pray for her son who had recently taken his own life." She sounded sad.

"I know you are a busy group, Sister. By the way, Mrs. Grenno's cancer is in remission. I think your prayers had something to do with it. Sister Theresa, I brought one of my brothers, Armando, to meet you."

I cringed at the sound of my name. It was okay listening to my brother talk with this nun, but now I'd have to say something.

"Wonderful!" Her voice sounded excited.

I leaned further back.

"I'm so pleased to meet you!" she said. "How old are you?"

"Ten," I said, barely loud enough to be heard.

"I have a ten-year-old nephew. He's in the fifth grade. Are you in the fifth?"

"Yes, ma'am."

"Where do you go to school?"

"St. Rita's Grammar School, ma'am."

"Oh my! The School Sisters of Notre Dame teach there, right?"

"Yes, ma'am."

"I understand they're a bit strict. Do you find them that way?"

"Sometimes, um, what's your room like?"

"Excuse me?"

"Your bedroom, what's it like?"

"Well, there's not much. I have a crucifix hanging on the wall, a cot, and a small chest of drawers. I need little space for clothes, since I am given only two habits; one to wear while I the launder other. There's a table with a pen and paper, a chair, and my prayer book."

"Do you pray a lot?"

I heard her chuckle softly.

"I guess you could say that. Everything we do is prayer. The many jobs and tasks we perform are done for the glory of God, like when we bake the unleavened bread that is made into the communion wafers you take in church. We also have formal group prayer sessions from early morning into the late hours."

"Do you pray more than my mother?"

She laughed.

PROFILE

I didn't understand what was so funny about my question?

"Well, I don't know. That's a good question. Maybe not! Your brother tells me your mother is good at praying. How about you? What do you like to do? Do you play sports?"

I sat up. "Yeah! I play baseball!"

"I love baseball. Do you play for a team?"

"My school. I pitch, catch, play right field, and second base."

"Wow, a good utility player. That's great!"

"Sister Theresa, he brought his mitt," Tony said.

"I'd love to see it if it's okay with you."

"Sure, I'd really like to show it to you. But how do I get in?"

She and Tony laughed.

"You can't go in," Tony said. "Put your mitt in the turn."

"In the what?"

Tony pointed to the wooden cylinder. "In there."

I set the glove in the center of it, and Tony gave it a slight push. It spun almost silently to the other side. I tried to catch a glimpse of her as it spun, but the design didn't allow even a peek.

"It's a Wilson," she said, "good make. And it's nearly broken-in. Have you oiled it yet?"

"No, Sister."

"Wash it with saddle soap and warm water, then wipe it with a rag. Then rub in leather oil really well. It'll stay malleable and keep it from drying out. Dryness weakens the leather."

I could hear her slapping leather. She must have put on the glove and was hitting it with her fist like I do when waiting to catch a fly ball.

The cylinder spun back around with the mitt in it. "It's a good mitt," she said. "Take good care of it, okay?"

I picked it up and put it on to see if I could feel the warmth of her hand. I smelled it to see if I could catch her scent. I noticed that my mitt was shaped to be round.

"See how I formed it?" she asked.

"Yeah, how'd you get it like that?"

"I loosened the laces and brought the wrist strap over to the tightest setting, like you'd tighten your belt. It'll help your hand fit snugly, and it gives the mitt that fan shape. Put your two middle fingers into the last finger of the glove with your index finger and pinkie at rest on the outside. Now the chances of a hard-hit ball hitting and hurting your hand is much less likely. Hit the middle fingers of the glove with your fist and catch like that. The mitt will trap the ball."

I hit the middle fingers of my mitt with my fist, and it nearly snapped shut around my hand. "Cool! How'd you know to do all of that?"

"I played a lot of baseball with my brothers when growing up. I also played for school and city teams. I was an all-star. My team even went to the state finals two seasons in a row."

I looked at Tony amazed. I set my mitt on the floor, leaned forward in my chair and put my hands and cheek against the wall. I wanted to get closer to her.

"And promise me you won't throw a ball hard until you've warmed up your arm. I have a brother who was a great baseball player. He was being scouted for the majors.

PROFILE

But once on a dare, he threw a rock as hard as he could at a bottle that was far away. His arm muscles weren't warmed up. Something snapped in his shoulder. He never threw well again. You must warm up before throwing hard, okay?"

"Yes, Sister, I sure will."

"Very good."

Tony leaned toward the wall. "Sister, we have to go now," he said.

I looked at him disappointed. I wanted to stay longer and tell her about me stealing home and winning a game for my team, but I knew better than to question Tony.

"Thank you so much for the visit. Will you come again?"

"Yeah, Sister, I'd really like to."

"Wonderful. I'll look forward to it."

I was filled with questions for Tony as we walked down the hillside stairs.

"Will she live in there for the rest of her life? Can she see her family? Can she watch TV?"

At the car I realized that I had forgotten my mitt. Tony sent me back to fetch it with strict warning not to disturb anyone. I made my way to the glove. My worn tennis shoes were as quiet as a pair of old socks on the shiny wooden floor.

"There it is," I whispered, seeing my mitt lying by the chair.

I grabbed it and walked back to the door. I carefully turned the doorknob and took a step out but stopped and looked back in from the threshold; one foot was in the peace-filled house, the other out in the echoing din of cars and trucks racing up and down the avenue below. It was so very still inside, a good still, a serene still. I wanted to sit on the floor to hear Sister's whispers and gentle walking on the other side of the wall, but Tony had the car running and waving me back down.

An emotion I didn't understand welled up in my chest. I felt like crying and whispered, "I want to stay with you, Sister Theresa."

PROFILE

Portrait of a Rose

Philip Kijawa, my best friend in the sixth grade, would be dead by the end of the day. He and his neighbor friend, Danny Cortez, would be crushed and suffocated under tons of rain-soaked earth. The police would pull their mud-slick bodies from the cave the two had been digging on weekends and after school. Philip's mother would not get his daily after-school phone call where she worked. She would call Danny's mother to see if the boys were together. But Danny wasn't home from school either, though he should have been.

It had rained for almost a week. Unusual in the semi-arid climate of San Diego where we lived. And it had been raining all that day.

The nuns didn't allow us to go out to the playground at recess time. They had a room monitor lead the class in an indoor game called Seven Up. The monitor chose seven kids to line up in the front of the room, while the rest of us laid our heads on our desktops and hid our eyes. The seven then walked around, touched someone's head, and returned to the front. We raised our heads and tried guessing which of the seven had touched us. If we guessed correctly, we got to take the kid's place. Lame!

Philip and I agreed that they were fools with no imaginations. Games were supposed to be fun, and this one wasn't even close to being fun. It was a stupid teacher's game, not ours.

Every time it rained Sister would ask, "What would you like to play class?" She smiled self-assuredly knowing that the indoctrinated would shout, "Seven Up! Seven Up!" Teachers liked the game because it was quiet play.

It rained the day Philip died, and we were playing Seven Up at recess time. Philip and I decided to spice it up a little by tripping the kid who walked down the aisle between our desks. Making contact with a kid's foot was one point. Making him stumble was two, and a fall-down was a five-point bingo.

Matthew would have fallen to the floor, but he caught himself on Ruth's desk and almost took her and her desk with him. We scored it four points. Now we were having real fun with our heads lowered while tripping kids passing our desks and hiding our laughter.

Philip and I became best friends at the beginning of the year when we were assigned desks next to each other. We came to realize that we liked impish humor.

He had a wide and high forehead that gave him the appearance of being bald. And he loved pulling pranks. Once, before school, while our class was waiting to go into church, he slipped on a set of large flesh-colored ears. Those standing behind him started laughing. He looked around as if wondering what the laughter was about. Even humorless Mother Superior couldn't help herself and chuckled when she told him to put them away. On another occasion he came to school with a nail through his finger. It was wrapped in gauze that was stained with dry blood.

"The doctor couldn't pull it out, see!" Philip tugged on the nail. "I've got another appointment to see him again tomorrow." It was too much of a distraction during class, and Sister made him take off the bandage and nail that was curved around his finger.

PROFILE

Philip wasn't the best of students, but he did have a curiosity and love of the natural world. Last year in fifth grade, he was excited because our teacher, Mrs. Balisarrio, introduced us to the natural sciences. She regularly brought cool specimens to class, like live reptiles in glass cases.

Philip worked hard for her and outdid the rest of us when it came to science projects. He once brought to class a one by one-and-a-half foot piece of plywood. He had mounted a landscape on it with miniature trees on a hillside and a lake made of clear blue plastic. Roaming all about it were dinosaurs. His was voted the best project. After that rainy day, there would be no more projects from Philip, and no more pranks.

I knelt in a pew with my twin brother, Fernando, and a classmate, Keith, at the funeral parlor where a memorial rosary was held the night before the funeral. Philip lay so very still in the casket. It didn't look like him, but a lifeless flesh-colored mannequin dressed in a dark suit.

At the end of the service, Keith suggested we go to Philip's parents and say we were sorry. I felt nervous about going but followed Keith. Philip's parents were sitting in the front pew. His mother had been sobbing and moaning through the entire service. She was dressed in black and sat leaning against her husband. She looked haggard and drained to the point of being sick.

"We're sorry Philip had to die," Keith whispered to her. She looked at us for a moment then put a hand on Keith's cheek.

All she could muster in a weak and trembling voice was, "You're nice boys." I stood staring at the odd spectacle of a grown-up completely depleted and vulnerable. Her soul had been ripped away from her.

That night at dinner my sister Martha said she had heard that Philip's mother had cursed the nuns, blaming them and the church for Philip's death.

"But it wasn't their fault," I said.

"Sister Cynthia said that Mrs. Kijawa isn't well because of her grief," Martha said. "Philip was her only child and we need to pray for her. Danny Cortez's father said he wasn't going to question God's will and that if God wanted one of his children, then he must obey as Abraham did with his son Isaac."

Fernando and I talked that night, lying in our bedroom. "He never told those silly snot jokes or played silly games with the girls like some of the other boys do," Fernando said.

"How could God allow this to happen?" I said. Neither of us said anything more.

All the next day I was preoccupied with Philip's death. I went to my neighbor Chris's house to see if he wanted to play. His mother invited me in and gave us cookies.

"I heard one of your schoolmates died recently."

"Yes, ma'am, he was my best friend in school. I wonder why God took him."

Chris's mother cupped my face in her hands and looked me in the eye. "I know that your family has certain beliefs, sweetheart, but some people see things differently. Some people aren't so sure there is a God."

My head spun with the very idea of not believing in God. *Didn't everybody know that He made us, and the world, and the entire universe?*

PROFILE

Chris's mom continued. "Whether or not a person believes in God, the same things will happen to them. Your religion teaches that a god created the world. But I believe that no one knows how it all happened. No matter, the world is a place in which all living things are designed to reproduce: people, animals, even plants. Everything is born, matures to reproduce, and dies. The reason for being created is to procreate and keep the life cycle going. Your poor friend's mother procreated, but her offspring will not, and she is suffering the greatest loss. The reason for her existence, for having known the joy and pain of motherhood, was stolen from her. Was it God who did this, or was it just a tragic fateful event that no one is responsible for? Who knows? What we know is that she will anguish and yen for her child to the end of her life. I can't think of a crueler irony than becoming a childless mother. Her baby was stolen from her. How could a merciful and loving God allow this to happen? I wish I had an answer."

I kept thinking for the rest of the day about what Chris's mom had said and decided I needed to take it up with Father McGuinn. Didn't God give Philip his curiosity and love of science? And that's what caused him to die!

Philip and Danny had been digging a cave in the canyon near their neighborhood. They were looking for rocks for a youth science fair. But their digging had produced few specimens and so they dug further in. Why did they crawl into the cave when it was raining? It would have been cold and damp. And how could a loving and merciful God allow this to happen? I lay haunted by the question while trying to sleep that night.

The next day during the funeral mass, Father McGuinn told the story of a gardener who took great pride in his work tending the grounds of an estate. One day he noticed that someone had stolen a perfect blossom from a prized rose bush. He became angry until he learned that the owner of the estate, so moved by the beauty of the flower, took it into the mansion to show it to his dinner guests. The gardener was pleased that the owner so appreciated his work.

We stood outside the church in the cold fog as the pallbearers loaded Philip's coffin onto the hearse after the funeral. The last image I had of him was when we were laughing after tripping kids during Seven Up. What was it going to be like without him sitting in the desk next to me ever again?

The hearse, followed by the black limousine with Philip's parents and a procession of cars, slowly pulled away and disappeared into the fog.

PROFILE

Lord, Snow, and Dawn

Tino began thinking of Lola, and how good it felt when she sat on the back of his motorcycle with her arms wrapped around him and her soft breasts pressed against his back. He was sure that she was the love of his life and one day they'd marry. But how could he support her? He wasn't all that good at holding down a job. *What about making a career out of the Marines after I join up?* he thought. *Marines don't get fired. Or maybe I could learn to be a mechanic from Rex the biker who we rode with in New Mexico. Rex hired guys like me who have a hard time making it in the regular world. There's good money in mechanics, and I could let my hair grow and dress however I want, and then ride motorcycles with Rex and his biker friends. Of course! That's it! I'll join the Marines, learn discipline, and earn my Pa's respect, then marry Lola and become an ace mechanic with Rex.* Tino's day brightened.

He rode with his head held high. He would show his parents and the rest of the doubters that he would not only succeed, but he'd do it his own way. He would become a great mechanic with a shop, and be like Rex helping young guys who'd gotten into trouble and give them a second chance, and on top of everything else, he'd have a beautiful wife! Tino began singing loudly, "Get your motor running, head out on the highway," when his bike began slowing on its own. He turned the accelerator grip and the tach needle jumped, but the bike didn't respond with its usual burst of speed. *Damn it! Now what?* It was as if the bike was in neutral. It kept slowing until it came to a stop. He looked on helplessly as Sal, his older brother, continued down the road. Tino dismounted and made a quick inspection. His bike's drive chain had disappeared.

Sal had ridden two miles before noticing that Tino wasn't behind him anymore. Sal pulled over and took a nervous look at his watch hoping Tino would soon appear. Sal waited a couple of minutes before he sighed and made a U-turn to head back. He found Tino leaning against his bike with his arms crossed.

"Lost my drive chain," Tino said. "I'll bet Pat didn't put it on right after his stupid prank. It's gotta be lying on the road somewhere back there."

"*Hijo de la…*" Sal said, then gunned his engine and doubled back with a close eye on the asphalt. Tino saw him stop a few hundred feet up the road, lean over, pick up the snake-like drive chain.

"What're we gonna do now?" Tino said as Sal pulled up.

"The master link's gone. There's gotta be a Honda dealer in the town we passed a while ago where I can get a new one. Be back as soon as I can." Sal sped off. A school bus converted into a motorized home and painted the colors of the rainbow approached in Tino's direction. *Humph, hippies*, he thought.

Tino stared at the bus as it drew near. "Peace and Love" was written in elaborate lettering in the space between the windshield and roof. The driver smiled and waved as he pulled over. His full, dark beard hung to the middle of his chest, and a thin leather strap, wrapped around his head, kept his shoulder-length hair from his face. Grace Slick's voice bellowed from an eight-track tape deck stereo system. "When the truth is found, to be lies…"

PROFILE

The hippie opened the door, slid out of the driver's seat, and landed on the ground with a bounce. "Having trouble, brother?" His bone-white collarless shirt with puffy sleeves hung over gray corduroy pants tucked into a pair of tan suede boots adorned with tassels that dangled as he walked.

"Nothing my brother and I can't fix," Tino said, feeling a little weird about talking with a guy who was dressed like some kind of wild gypsy. "He went to get a part for my bike. But thanks for stopping."

"We are called to serve," Tassels said. "Too bad about your ride, man."

The double doors of the bus swung open. A pretty young woman descended the steps. Her milk-white skin was a stark contrast to her shining black hair that hung long and straight past her waist. A tan leather vest fit snuggly over her silky deep blue blouse. Her moccasins were barely visible beneath a long, chocolate brown skirt that swept the earth as she walked. A thin halo of silver ribbon entwined with tiny dried yellow flowers rested on the crown of her head. She appeared to hover over the ground like a saint Tino had seen in a religious movie. She floated toward Tassels, stopped next to him, and set her head against his shoulder.

"Been on the road long, brother?" Tassels asked.

"Since California."

"Far out, man! I can't imagine spending that much time with anyone in *my* family."

"It's got its ups and downs," Tino said. "But mostly ups." He nodded toward the bus. "How's it traveling in that thing?"

"It's groovy, man. We've got everything we need."

"Would you like to see it?" the Saint asked.

"Yeah, I really would," Tino said.

The Saint and Tino climbed the steps. Tassels walked around to the rear of the bus. The dull-sweet odor of burned incense greeted Tino as he entered. Sitting on a wooden rocking chair behind the driver's seat was a petite girl who couldn't have been much past fifteen.

"This is my baby sister, Dawn," the Saint said. The girl in the chair raised her head only long enough to give a cursory smile, then got back to sewing a brightly colored patch of a mushroom to the cuff of a pair of well-worn jeans.

"Dawn's sewing Lord's pants."

"Lord?" Tino asked.

"Our man."

"That's a pretty interesting name," Tino said thinking it funny and heretical.

"He's an interesting man."

The Saint took a step toward Tino so her face was inches from his. He felt uneasy and took a half step back. She shifted and pressed her hip to his. His heart started pounding. He felt as though her dark doe-like eyes were seeing through him.

She cooed, "I'm Snow."

"Snow! That's a cool name."

She then extended her hand in a broad stroke, inviting Tino to admire the world they had created inside the bus. He looked around trying to appear as if he was more interested in the décor than her advances.

A portable stove for camping sat on a narrow counter, its green paint was faded and chipping. Hand-thrown ceramic plates and cups filled a small sink. Tino noticed that they were standing on the hide of a large animal. Tino squatted and ran his fingers over it. It felt soft and smooth. Blankets and pillows in blue and green paisley patterns lay over a large mattress to the rear. A guitar case leaned against a wall beside a tambourine. On the ceiling in glittering gold and outlined in deep blue was a huge peace sign with "It is possible" written over it.

"This is really bitchen," Tino said.

Snow smiled warmly and looked into his eyes. "Life is beautiful."

Tino's heart jumped. Why was she coming on to him with her man Lord just outside?

Lord climbed the stairs and entered the bus with a leather pouch in his hand and set it on the counter. He ignored Tino and Snow as they looked on. He took a pack of cigarette rolling papers from his shirt pocket, pull one out, and set it flat on the counter. He opened the pouch and took out a pinch of a green leafy substance and spread it along the center of the paper.

Holy shit! Tino thought. "Is that marijuana?"

Lord looked up smiling. "Well, it sure ain't tobacco."

"I've heard of it but have never seen the stuff."

Lord then rolled a near perfect cigarette in seconds. He ran the edge of the paper across his tongue to seal it and twisted the ends. He held it up looking at Tino with raised eyebrows. "Care to partake?"

"No, thanks. I'm not into dope."

"How do you know, man? Ever try it?"

"No."

"Then how do you know?"

"I guess I don't, but I'm afraid that it'll lead to harder stuff."

"Aw man, that's the man's propaganda. It just ain't so. How do you get high?"

"Beer, when I can get it."

"This ain't nearly as hard as that shit, man. That stuff'll kill you. I've tried just about every drug there is, and alcohol was the hardest on my body. I always felt like I got beat up after drinking." He lifted the joint and raised his eyebrows again, smiling impishly.

Tino was softening. *He's right. I don't know what it's like, and if I tried it who'd ever know?* He looked at Lord, then at Snow, "Oh, what the hell."

"Well alright, man!" Lord said. Snow giggled and clapped her hands.

"Why're you so happy about me getting high?"

"Because you're converting to the light," Snow said.

Tino looked at her askew.

Lord struck a stick match against the counter and lit the joint. He closed his eyes as he sucked on it, slow and hard. His face turned red. He handed the joint to Tino.

Tino tentatively raised the joint to his lips. "What do you mean by 'converting to the light'?" He imitated Lord and took a deep hit, but the harsh smoke tore at his lungs and he broke out into a coughing fit. He hacked out every bit of what he had inhaled and then some. The hippies burst into laughter. He passed it to Snow, still coughing. She took a much smaller hit, held it in and handed the joint down to Dawn, in her chair. Snow exhaled. "Ever hear of Timothy Leary and his church?"

"Yeah, he's the guy who keeps getting busted for using drugs."

"First of all, Timothy Leary's a *researcher* in psychedelic therapy at Harvard University," Lord said, offended that someone would reduce his guru to an addict. "Secondly, he's a teacher with a new and beautiful message, like Jesus. Timothy Leary has seen the light that all men..."

"And women," Snow added.

"That all men *and* women seek. He founded a church called The League for Spiritual Discovery. We are living his mantra: turn on, tune in, and drop out. We're on our way to San Francisco. I've wanted to go there since I heard about the Summer of Love there last year. After that we're going to join up with Leary and his church. They've declared lysergic acid diethylamide as their sacrament."

"Declared what?"

"Lysergic acid diethylamide. L-S-D, man."

"You gotta be kidding. They're using a drug as a communion host?" Now, Tino was offended.

"You don't understand. LSD isn't just a drug, man. It's a portal. A portal to the other side, a way to see, you know? A way to really and truly see. Try some and you'll understand."

Lord stared at Tino, studying him for a second. He then stepped to the glove compartment of the bus and took out a box of Kodak film. He removed the small gray canister and peeled off the lid, and tapped out what appeared to be tiny square pieces of shiny black film. He picked up a copy of a *National Geographic* magazine, opened it, and tore out a page with a photograph of ancient Mayan glyphs. Lord took a single-edge razor blade and cut a three-inch square containing a glyph of a stylized snake. He then carefully folded one of the flecks of film into the paper. He looked up at Tino. "God forbade Adam and Eve to eat of the forbidden fruit."

"Are you saying God didn't want Adam and Eve to trip-out on LSD?" Tino said.

Snow and Dawn giggled.

Lord ignored them. "I'm going to explain something to you, man." He motioned Tino to sit on a chair next to the driver's seat. Tino sat, feeling a little nervous. *What was this guy up to?* Lord sat in the driver's seat and turned to stare into Tino's eyes. He spoke slowly and deliberately. "LSD has the same effect as mushrooms."

"Mushrooms?" Tino said. "What do mushrooms have to do with anything?"

"Not just mushrooms, man. I'm talking about sacred mushrooms, psilocybin mushrooms. They'll expand your mind in ways you could never imagine. For me, it was the first time in my life I could see, I mean really and truly see, man. It wasn't LSD Adam and Eve were not to eat. It was psilocybin mushrooms. They helped them to understand so much more than their mortal minds ever could on their own. LSD has the same effect. You'll get it when you use it." He held up the small packet. "Do it when you're in a mellow mood, and do it in a place where you feel safe. And don't let it get wet or it'll lose its power."

"You mean this isn't film, but LSD?"

"It's a beautiful thing, isn't it? The pigs never suspect."

Lord placed the packet into Tino's hand. Tino was overcome with an ominous feeling that he should not accept the offering. A deep curiosity gnawed at him. He slipped it into his coin pocket. *I'll toss it when I get back on the road.* "Is it like getting drunk?"

"Naw, man, nothin' like that. There's an intense ride up, kind of jittery. Some people don't like it, but it's fun if you're head's in the right place. Next you'll peak, your mind will expand, and you'll see as you've never seen before. And then there's a peaceful ride down."

Tino rose from the chair. "It's cool how you can hide this from the cops, but how do you hide the pot? Don't you get stopped and pulled over and searched, especially riding around in this bus."

Lord stood. "It's been a major hassle, man. It's another reason we're going to California. It's mellower out there. We've been on the road two weeks, and the heat's pulled us over three times! They look inside the bus, but never under it," he laughed. "And I've got stuff to sell in sealed cans with Campbell's soup labels. And it's mm, mm good!"

"It's going to be groovy when we get to California," Snow said. "Is it as cool as they say it is?"

"Heck, I don't know," Tino said. "It's just home to me. Maybe it's a little easier in San Francisco where the hippies are taking over." Tino felt relaxed from the marijuana. "I love it that you guys are so free. You're lucky. My folks would never allow me do this. Are your parents okay with it?"

"My once self was called Jethro Cornelius Taylor III," Lord said. "And Jethro was born to a confused rich man who married a confused Southern belle. The rich man got into politics and now votes to keep 'the nigras in their place,' as he says, and he supports dropping napalm and Agent Orange in Viet Nam. And the government thinks I'm going to register for the draft. Ha! I reject that life, all of it, even to the name given to me by agents of an oppressive society. I am 'Lord.' And Lord has discovered that love and peace are the way. We need to make love, not war, man." Snow and Dawn smiled warmly as they looked up at him. Lord put an alligator clip on the shortened joint, took a drag, and then passed it to Tino.

Tino looked at Snow and Dawn. "What about you guys? Aren't your parents worried about you?" Dawn pursed her lips hiding pain.

"We're not even sure they even know we're gone," Snow said. "We're the last of their sixteen children what live in the West Virginie Mountains. Mama dances with snakes and drinks poison as her worship, and Pap drinks as much shine as he stills. A man who be drinkin' that devil water does regretful things to his people, an' even worse to them who would cross him. Most of his young-uns have gone off to live with neighbors or hitched up with somebody to our likin' or just done disappeared like me and Dawn."

"That's sad," Tino said thinking it strange how her person changed when she talked about her family. "It's very sad," he said. He held up the clip and studied what little there was left of the joint. "It's making me feel really relaxed. I wish I could always feel like this."

"You're a good dude," Lord said. "Come with us. There's no church, no hassle, just love, happiness, and insight."

Snow neared Tino again and spoke softly. "This life's a whole lot more to my likin'. It's a free life, a free life to live and do what I want, and when I want." She leaned against him and brushed her breasts against his arm. She looked into his eyes. "Do y'all believe in free love?"

Tino's head spun. "Sounds wonderful."

"I think I'd surely like to fuck ya'll right now," she said.

Naked lust overcame Tino. He felt an erection coming on.

PROFILE

"We can give you privacy," Lord said, "or the four of us can have a love fest."

Tino shook his head. "I could never do it in a group."

"Say no more, brother," Lord said and reached for Dawn's hand, helping her from the rocker. "Everything in our world is free man, free in every way."

Snow, still gazing into Tino's eyes, put her hand on his crotch and rubbed it gently. "Let's have a beautiful time."

Tino trembled with want, but Lola came to his mind. "I'm in love with someone," he said softly.

Snow's eyes flooded with tears. "And ya want to be true to her. That's a beautiful thing," she whispered, "a real beautiful thing."

Lord put his hand on Tino's shoulder. "No hassle, man. Why don't you come along with us? Shed your old life. Live free, truly free. Get high when you want and make beautiful love, if and when you want."

"I'd surely like that," Snow said.

Make love anytime, Tino thought. *Get high anytime, no school, no church, no hassles.* Movement toward the back of the bus caught Tino's eye. He looked out the rear window. A small dark-skinned man on a motorcycle in the distance was coming toward them fast. "Holy shit! My brother!"

The hippies looked out the window that framed Sal as he approached.

"Your brother wouldn't be cool with this?" Lord said.

"Cool with this? He's a Catholic priest!"

"Wow. Major bummer, man."

"He accepts people, he's cool like that. But there's no way he'd be okay with me getting stoned."

The three hippies looked concerned for Tino and ushered him out of the bus.

Lord smiled at Sal as he pulled up and stopped. Sal narrowed his eyes, assessing the situation.

"How're you folks doing? You've been visiting with my brother?" He scanned the hippies. *What could his little brother be up to now?*

"We're doing good, Sal," Tino said, trying to sound casual. He pointed to the bus. "You ought to see the inside, it's really cool."

Lord took a step forward. "Nice to meet you, man." He raised his palm, greeting Sal in the form of an American Indian. "I. Am. Lord."

"Lord?" Sal said amused. "Well, I've been wanting to meet you for a heck of a long time!"

"It's my enlightened name!"

"That's very interesting. Why Lord?"

"Because I Lord over myself. I am the 'I am, who am,' of my life, and of my destiny. I reject the culture of consumption that destroys the spirit of men."

"And women," said Snow.

"You're a deep thinker," Sal said.

Lord gave Sal a hard, cold stare. "I have learned to see."

Tino, sensing a pissing contest between alpha males, intervened. "Sal, they stopped to help when they saw me pulled over."

Sal glanced at Tino and then at the hippies, and took a conciliatory tone. "Well, it's much appreciated." He pulled a small plastic bag from his pocket. "Found a master link, *hermano*. The mechanic said it's not unusual for them to wear out and pop off."

PROFILE

Sal took the drive chain, a set of pliers from his tool kit, and knelt next to Tino's bike.

Lord turned and hugged Tino. "Have a safe trip, man. It was real meeting you." He turned to Sal. "You got a good brother, man."

Dawn smiled and nodded a goodbye at Tino. Snow stepped to him and kissed him on the cheek. "I hope I'll see you in California," she said sadly. She turned and followed Lord and Dawn onto the bus. Lord started the engine, pulled onto the road, and waved as they passed. Tino waved back. A bumper sticker on the back of the bus read, "Make Love Not War." Sal finished with the drive chain and stood. The brothers watched the bus get smaller as it headed down the road.

"Looks like you made quite an impression on them," Sal said.

"I guess so. I wonder if they're really as happy as they're making out to be."

"Hard to say," Sal said. "My guess is that they're trying to convince themselves as much as the rest of us that they've found *the way*."

"Say," Tino said. "You wouldn't have something sweet to eat stashed in your gear, would you?"

"Hungry?"

"Kind of. I just feel like having something sweet and crunchy like Oreo cookies or rocky road ice cream. Know what I mean?"

"Yeah, that'd be great, but you can forget about eating right now. We've got a lot of time to make up." Sal fired up his bike, and hit the road with a vengeance.

Tino followed him, nursing a case of the munchies.

Love at First Sight

"You don't have to tell me your name," he said, walking up to the bench where she sat. "You fit the description to a tee."

She smiled. "And so do you, except that you are even more handsome than I imagined."

"And you're more beautiful than I could have imagined."

"Why did you suggest we meet in the Healdsburg Plaza?" she asked.

"Because it's where one should fall in love."

Her eyes flooded with tears. Without a thought, she leapt to her feet, cupped his cheeks in her hands, and kissed his lips. "Oh my goodness!" she said. "I've never done such a thing. I'm just beside myself!"

He felt a powerful stir in his loins. "It's meant to be. Just let it happen," he said. "My heart is beating so hard it's scary."

"And so is mine."

Their hands met, connecting the strange, yet wonderful, electricity buzzing through them. Their fingers meshed, and they began a slow stroll unable to keep their eyes from gazing at each other. His voice quavered, "Do you believe in love at first sight?"

"Yes, yes I do, but I fell more in love with you each time we spoke online. Your being so handsome is only the icing on such a delicious cake." He stopped in mid-stride, whirled her around, and pressed his lips to hers surprising himself. And she allowed it, a willing partner in this unabashed public display, so unlike her usually shy self.

PROFILE

She wrapped her arms around his neck and kissed him, drinking in his very soul. Fate was a wondrous gift that had come to them, straight from the quiver of Eros.

She drew back and purred, "I've never been more sure of myself; I, I love you Kirk."

"What?"

"I said. I love you, Kirk."

"Kirk? Who's Kirk?"

"Kirk! Kirk Armstrong! The man who loves to snuggle by a winter fire. The man who loves walks on the beach, and intelligent women and cats, same as me!"

"Cats? I hate cats! And my name is Bob! I'm getting a feeling that you're not Brandy. The chick who loves the Forty-Niners, Budweiser, and Sunday afternoons at the sports bar."

"Brandy? My name's Aurora, thank you very much! And, football? It's brutal. I hate football!"

"No you don't."

"Yes, I do."

"Do not."

"Do so. And Budweiser? Paleese! Do I look like a barfly to you?"

He glared at her. "Next thing you know you're going to tell me you're one of those Merlot-sipping wine snobs who sends money to public radio."

"But I love Terry Gross!"

"Oprah?"

"Even more!"

"Eat meat?"

"Vegetarian!"

STORIES

IT IS SAID THAT TO ERR IS HUMAN but to really screw things up takes a computer. Who would have guessed that the two did wind up falling in love after such a rocky start? They decided it would have been a shame to waste a Saturday evening, and they should at least try to get to know each other. By the end of the night they had polished off a pitcher of beer at the local sports bar (or rather, he did; she couldn't finish half a glass). Afterward they shared a dinner al fresco. She had a glass of Merlot, he another two bottles of Bud.

They married the following year at the Catholic Church to comply with his parents' wishes. The wedding was soon followed by a seaside ceremony at the coast to satisfy Aurora's pagan leanings. Bob hunts on weekends, as he always had. Aurora continues to volunteer at the pet hospital.

Bob and Aurora named their son Bob after Bob's father and mother, Bob and Bobette. The boy's middle name is River, after the Russian.

Aurora secretly loved being with a man who had primal tendencies. Bob was grateful to have been relieved of trying to live up to playing the role of a super-macho.

Note:
A second couple, Norm and Norma, had found each other online as well and had managed to find each other on the same night, and on the same bench in the plaza, as Bob and Aurora. Norma had been sitting on the opposite end. They shared common interests and tastes in food, music, and art and soon married, but divorced the following year citing irreconcilable differences.

Acknowledgments

This book would not have come to pass had it not been for Waights Taylor. Not only was it his idea for me to put this collection together, his encouragement and patience were invaluable. *Muchas gracias, mi amigo.*

I also am indebted to the fine writers whose work I so respect and admire for taking precious time from the demands of their personal lives, work, and writing schedules to review and comment on my work.

Al Young is an internationally acclaimed novelist and California Poet Laureate Emeritus.

David Beckman is a novelist, poet, and playwright. His plays have been staged in New York City, Los Angeles, and Santa Rosa. He also authored the novel *Under Pegasus*.

Ianthe Brautigan is the author of *You Can't Catch Death: A Daughter's Memoir.*

Jonah Raskin, prolific Sonoma County writer, has authored enough books to fill a shelf in my writing studio. In researching his book on Jack London, Jonah came across a London quote, "I have been writing like a tiger all day." Jonah must be descended from the same litter.

Susan Swartz, author of *Juicy Tomatoes, Ripe Living after 50*, is a radio commentator and columnist for the *Press Democrat*.

A final thanks to my editor, Arlene Miller, for focusing her editorial eye on my work to make it presentable.

About the Author

Armando García-Dávila burst upon the Sonoma County literary world in the latter part of the 1990s. What started as a series of op. ed. pieces he wrote concerning the First Persian Gulf War and the memories of friends killed in the Vietnam War, turned to poetry to express wide ranging thoughts rooted in his Mexican-American/Catholic upbringing. To make clear his humble background, he called himself the "blue-collar" poet.

Newspaper columnist Ray Holley wrote at the time, "Be sure to check out Armando. . . . (while) you still have a chance to see him in an intimate setting before he becomes justly famous for his work."

His poems have been widely published and also found their way into union newsletters and Sunday pulpits. He has read his poetry to immigrant laborers in the vineyards and prisoners in San Quentin. In 2002, he was chosen as the Healdsburg Literary Laureate.

Armando's biggest supporters are his wife, Kathy, his two grown children, Cecilia and Emilio, and his twin brother, Fernando.

www.ingramcontent.com/pod-product-compliance
Lightning Source LLC
Chambersburg PA
CBHW070459100426
42743CB00010B/1681